This book is dedicated to the memory of Michael Bruno,
colleague, teacher, and friend.

Distributive Justice and Economic Development

Development and Inequality in the Market Economy

The purpose of this series is to encourage and foster analytical and policy-oriented work on market-based reform in developing and postsocialist countries. Special attention will be devoted in the series to exploring the effects of free market policies on social inequality and sustainable growth and development.

Editor:
Andrés Solimano

Editorial Board:
Alice Amsden
François Bourguignon
William Easterly
Patricio Meller
Vito Tanzi
Lance Taylor

Titles in the Series:

Andrés Solimano, Editor. *Road Maps to Prosperity: Essays on Growth and Development*

Andrés Solimano, Editor. *Social Inequality: Values, Growth, and the State*

Lance Taylor, Editor. *After Neoliberalism: What Next for Latin America?*

Andrés Solimano, Eduardo Aninat, and Nancy Birdsall, Editors. *Distributive Justice and Economic Development: The Case of Chile and Developing Countries*

Distributive Justice and Economic Development

The Case of Chile and Developing Countries

Andrés Solimano, Eduardo Aninat, and Nancy Birdsall, Editors

Ann Arbor

THE UNIVERSITY OF MICHIGAN PRESS

A CIP catalog record for this book is available from the British Library.

Library of Congress Cataloging-in-Publication Data

Distributive justice and economic development : the case of Chile and
developing countries / Andrés Solimano, Eduardo Aninat, and Nancy
Birdsall, editors.
     p. cm — (Development and inequality in the market economy)
   Includes bibliographical references and index.
   ISBN 0-472-11086-1 (cloth : alk. paper)
   1. Economic development — Social aspects.   2. Economic
development — Social aspects — Chile.   3. Chile — Economic
policy.   4. Chile — Economic conditions — 1988.   5. Distributive
justice.   I. Solimano, Andrés.   II. Aninat, Eduardo.   III. Birdsall,
Nancy.   IV. Series
HD75.D576 2000   99-052800
338.9′009172′4 — dc21

Chapter 3 originally published in *Income Distribution and High-Quality
Growth* edited by Vito Tanzi and Ke-Young Chu (Cambridge: MIT
Press, 1998), 117–46. Copyright © 1998, MIT Press. Reprinted by
permission.

Preface

This book, focusing on issues of distributive justice and economic development, deals with the quest for policies that foster growth, prosperity, and material welfare and that are at the same time compatible with the ideals of social justice. These are the main thematic concerns of the Development and Inequality in the Market Economy series, published by the University of Michigan Press, of which this book is a new addition.

This volume is the result of a collaborative, policy-oriented, intellectual effort among high-rank cabinet members of the Chilean Government of President Eduardo Frei Ruiz-Tagle (1994–2000) in charge of the design and implementation of economic and social policies in Chile in the second half of the 1990s, scholars in the field of economic development, and senior-level officials from the World Bank, Inter-American Development Bank, and International Monetary Fund.

We are also honored to include in this volume one of the last pieces written by the late Michael Bruno, an enlightened person, pioneer scholar, and policymaker in the fields of economic development, inequality, and, later in his life, economic stabilization. Michael held important positions at the Central Bank of Israel and at the World Bank during his career. Beyond this, he exerted a very significant intellectual influence through his writings, advice, and warm personality in the development community at large.

We would also like to acknowledge the support provided by Margarita Caro and Diana Cortijo at the World Bank in the preparation of this book. The support of Ellen McCarthy and the excellent editorial work by Alja Kooistra at the University of Michigan Press are greatly appreciated.

Contents

CHAPTER 1

Introduction and Synthesis

Andrés Solimano

The relationship between the process of creating wealth (economic growth) and distributing it (social equity) has been a subject of great analytical and policy interest to development economists for many years. Is there an inevitable conflict, or tradeoff, between wealth creation and wealth distribution? Can both growth and social equity increase simultaneously? How does public policy affect growth-equity outcomes? These questions are particularly salient both for Latin America, where inequality levels are among the highest in the world, and for developing countries in general. Moreover, a question of key importance is to what extent market-oriented reform, followed with great impetus in the 1990s in the development and postsocialist world, is compatible with socially accepted patterns of distribution of income, wealth, and opportunities. A theme like this requires a dialogue between professional economists, social thinkers, and policy practitioners at both the national and international levels. This book aims at such a dialogue on issues of social equity, distributive justice, and economic development.

Part I provides the analytical-empirical perspective. It explores alternative concepts of distributive justice and social equity and their links with macropolicies, structural reform, and human development. The growth-equity relationship is explored at both the analytical and empirical levels by examining international experiences, including those of Latin America and other developing regions. The case of East Asia until the 1997–98 economic crisis is considered to be the benchmark of both rapid growth and improved social equity. Part II of the book is written mainly by policymakers, in this case several cabinet members (and some advisers) of the Chilean government of President Eduardo Frei (1994–2000). Economic reform in Chile, along free market lines, started in the mid-1970s under a military regime and was endorsed, with a new emphasis on social equity, in the 1990s by the democratic regime. During the 1990s, Chile experienced very rapid economic growth and significant poverty reduction, although there was still persistent wealth and income inequality. In light of recent analytical contributions and country experiences, this book addresses how economic growth can be more compatible, in Latin America and elsewhere, with the goals of equity and social justice as the main features of a socially oriented development strategy.

Analytical Perspectives and International Evidence

Concepts of Equity and Distributive Justice

To address some of the questions posed in this book, one must first define what is meant by "social equity." We can define three alternative concepts of social equity: (1) the absence of income deprivation for everybody in society (in this case social equity is identified with the reduction, or eventually the elimination, of poverty); (2) the absence of "large" inequalities of income or wealth; and (3) equality of opportunity. From the second perspective, equality of outcomes such as income and wealth is the focus, whereas in the third view more equitable access to opportunities for material progress and human fulfillment is sought.

A more in-depth understanding of the concept of social equity requires going back to the philosophical and economic foundations of the theory of distributive justice (see chap. 2 and Solimano 1998). The theory of distributive justice explores the causes and types of equality by distinguishing between background factors (wealth, talent, social connections) that condition wealth distribution, but are often beyond individual control, and elements pertaining to the realm of individual responsibility (effort, risk taking, ambition). From the perspective of philosophical theory, the distinction is made between "morally arbitrary factors" (background conditions) and conditions under the control of an individual, pertaining thus to the realm of personal freedom and individual autonomy (see Roemer 1996, 1998). Interestingly, although observed inequality is the result of both sets of determining factors, each set carries different ethical and moral implications for the nature of observed inequality in society. The theory of distributive justice is particularly illuminating as a means of clarifying the choice between equity of outcomes versus equality of opportunities and provides a conceptual basis for clarifying the ultimate goals of social policy.

Growth and Equity: Traditional and New Perspectives

Conventional wisdom holds that a tradeoff exists between the achievement of rapid growth and the reduction of income inequality. The two most common explanations given for the view that an unequal distribution of income is necessary for, or the likely consequence of, rapid economic growth, at least during some period, are the classical savings hypothesis and the Kuznets curve. First, the classical savings hypothesis, used by Nicholas Kaldor in his growth models, argued that since a high level of savings is a prerequisite for rapid growth in a capitalist society income must be concentrated in the hands of rich capitalists, whose marginal propensity to save is relatively high with respect to that of other economic groups.[1] Second, Kuznets (1955) observed that during the development process labor shifts from a low-productivity sector (traditional agriculture) to a high-productivity sector (manufacturing) and therefore economy-wide income inequality must initially increase if it is to later decrease as income per capita rises during the course of economic development.

During the 1990s, many economists have come to question this perceived tradeoff. In contrast, several explanations have been given for the positive relationship between growth and equity. First, increased equity can stimulate growth by increasing political and macroeconomic stability, as distributive conflict is less acute in more egalitarian societies. The chief channel here is the positive effect of a more stable economic and political environment on private capital formation, a key determinant of the rate of economic growth. Second, a more egalitarian distribution of income and/or access to education and credit are likely to boost the savings capacity and investment opportunities of the poor, which in turn will have a positive impact on growth, reversing the traditional Kaldorian story, which is centered on the differential class-based saving behavior of capitalists and workers. Third, a positive correlation between growth and equity can be explained by a variable such as (broad-based) education, which enhances both growth and equity. Fourth, in models in which aggregate demand affects long-run growth and effective demand increases with a rise in labor's share of national income, a more progressive distribution of income (toward labor) will accelerate economic growth.

As the previous discussion suggests, several arguments and theories question the traditional concept of an unavoidable tradeoff between growth and equity or more generally between economic development and distributive justice. From a policy perspective, it is important to note that the two variables can, under appropriate conditions, be mutually reinforcing. Policies that can set in motion a virtuous cycle of rapid growth with reduced inequality must act at several levels. At the macrolevel, maintaining fiscal and financial stability is essential to foster high investment and rapid growth. In fact, abundant empirical evidence already documents the positive effect of a stable macroframework of low inflation, fiscal balance, and financial stability on private capital accumulation. At macro- and microlevels, social policies should foster equal access, by the rural and urban poor and by workers and the middle class, to quality education, credit, land, and other productive assets. Progressive social policies also may include the redistribution of assets such as land, a democratic distribution of claims on the national capital stock, say, after privatization. This can be accomplished through schemes of vouchers distributed, as entitlements, to the population at large or through other policies.

The Kuznets story is questioned in chapter 3 by Michael Bruno, Martin Ravallion, and Lyn Squire. These authors bring new evidence to bear on the question of the relationship between growth and income distribution and poverty. Using newly constructed time series of country data on income distribution, the authors conclude that there is no clear tradeoff between growth and distribution. Moreover, based on their new data they argue for no systematic relationship between the mean rate of growth of income and its pattern of distribution. Bruno, Ravallion, and Squire maintain that while rapid growth seems not to be associated with worsening income distribution it does reduce absolute poverty. The authors show that the gains to the poor from growth will be lower the higher the initial level of asset inequality. They argue also that providing the poor with access to productive assets is an important means of achieving higher growth and reducing inequality.

The Social Impact of Crisis in the 1980s and 1990s

The debt crisis of the 1980s in Latin America led to a sharp and protracted decline in economic growth and living standards, particularly for low-income groups. Faced with the need to impose fiscal discipline, governments were forced (or chose) to reduce spending on education, health, infrastructure, and other items. Social programs were slashed and positive per capita growth disappeared in the 1980s in most of Latin America. New evidence indicates that the medium-run costs of reduced social spending may be high, as the effort to create human capital slowed sharply during the years of protracted adjustment and austerity. It can be argued that reduced social spending may hinder long-term growth in Latin America through the deterioration of education and health and an increase in poverty and inequality. So besides the growth-retarding effects of a slower pace of human capital formation we have to add the related negative impact of inequality on growth. The social impact of adjustment is also a relevant topic for the 1990s. Mexico suffered from a severe crisis in 1994–95, which cut real wages and increased unemployment and underemployment; in turn, the social effect on Latin America of the international crisis of 1998 remains to be determined. In chapter

4, Lance Taylor challenges the "Washington consensus" regarding the impact of stabilization and structural adjustment programs on social welfare and human development. Taylor offers a variety of policy recommendations for creating a positive linkage between growth and equity and for making stabilization and adjustment more benign, if not more beneficial, for the poor. For example, he emphasizes (1) the need to avoid sharp policy shocks, which have the greatest negative impact on low-income people through reduced employment and the decline in real wages; (2) the need to protect social expenditures during adjustment programs and to target social investment; and (3) the need to make social and gender equity and environmental quality central in the design and implementation of growth and development policies.

Social Commitments, Public Finance, and the State

A classic role of the state is to provide social protection to vulnerable groups (the children, the elderly, the disabled) and promote social equity and fairness. This, in turn, reflects the social commitments of society that are articulated through the political process. The state is the "agent" that implements mandates from the "principal," say, the electorate or the people. There is a growing literature showing the difficulties and failures of states to implement popular mandates in social policy and other areas. These difficulties originate at several levels. First, often it is difficult to achieve both a consensus on the priority given to the social agenda in the overall development strategy and the precise objectives of social policy. For example, should social policy be restricted to reducing poverty or should it also include redistributive policies? How is equality of opportunity to be defined? Second, once social priorities are established, a key issue is to design and implement adequate social policies that respect macrofinancial constraints and are effective in reaching the intended beneficiary groups. Third, an important issue is how to provide mechanisms of public accountability within the governments implementing these policies.

In chapter 5, Vito Tanzi addresses the issue of how governments can effectively undertake mandates of income redistribution and social protection. He argues that, while in theory public expenditures can have a positive impact on income distribution, the evidence shows that most government spending has been captured by the middle and upper classes in Latin America, a trend that he shows was present both in the 1960s and the 1980s. Tanzi makes several straightforward recommendations about how to better concentrate public expenditures on the poor and make the system of tax administration more efficient and fair. However, he admits that, while the recommendations sound fine in principle, their implementation may be very difficult in Latin America and elsewhere without adequate institutional and political reform oriented toward improving the quality, transparency, and accountability of fiscal policy.

Chapter 9 by José Pablo Arellano, former budget director, examines how a consistent policy of fiscal balance (or even surplus) followed in Chile in the 1990s has been compatible with social policies oriented toward reducing poverty and increasing the equality of opportunity through better and wider education and other social policies.

Education, Humanization of Work, and Second-Generation Social Policies

There is agreement that the provision of good quality education to low-income groups and popular classes is an important mechanism for the equalization of opportunity across the population. Chilean social policies in the second half of the 1990s have placed great importance on educational reform. This reform has increased the share of GDP devoted to education. It seeks to renew and modernize school curricula, improve the physical infrastructure of schools, retrain teachers, and create a system of "schools of excellence" in low-income neighborhoods in urban and rural areas. This effort aims to upgrade the educational profile of the young population to put it in line with economic modernization and improve the chances for economic progress and upward mobility of low-income people in Chile. Chapter 7, by Finance Minister Eduardo Aninat, and chapter 10, by former Education Minister Sergio Molina, elaborate on the rationale and expected effect on the equalization of opportunity and growth of educational reform in Chile.

The role of social institutions in the labor market is another important theme. Recent discussions have emphasized the need to deregulate the labor market and make it more flexible in light of the requirements of globalization and market-oriented reform. However, the social effects of "deregulating labor" should not be neglected. "Labor" is fundamentally different from "commodities" even in a capitalist economy that tends to "commodify" most social relations (Marx 1970; Polyani 1957). Historically, in the development of capitalism, labor unions and working class movements have played an important role in setting social agendas in the society at large and in seeking job security and other benefits for the working class and other vulnerable groups. However, market reform and globalization have challenged the "social labor contract" of the preglobalization era. The lack of protection from unemployment and macroeconomic volatility can be very detrimental to productivity and the quality of labor relations at both the firm and public sector levels. In fact, increased labor market flexibility should be complemented by labor protection measures such as unemployment insurance, labor training centers, and minimum income support schemes. Chapter 11, by former Labor Minister Jorge Arrate, discusses these and other issues in the context of Chilean labor policies, stressing the need to rebalance labor-capital relations in Chile (viewed as strongly pro-business during the Pinochet regime) and to "humanize" labor. Clearly, more work is needed on this theme of how to make labor more meaningful in market economies prone to volatility and job insecurity. Second-generation social policies must put more emphasis on labor market policies that go beyond flexibility. The "humanization of the workplace" in times of social fragmentation and uncertainty concerning the duration of labor contracts and general job instability, phenomena connected to globalization, is another concern of second-generation social policies.

Empirical Evidence and Regional Patterns

Empirical analysis of international experiences is playing an important role in the debate on the relationship between growth and equality. In recent years, many researchers have examined the experience of the East Asian economies, where rapid growth has been accompanied by declining income inequality, in search of the factors that can create a positive relationship between the processes of wealth creation and wealth distribution. These analyses have often pointed to the pursuit of more egalitarian wealth distribution policies, such as land reform, and policies intended to foster physical and human capital formation (e.g., through domestic savings mobilization, education, and training) as the key to their success. Other factors in the success of East Asia have been the maintenance of macroeconomic stability, export promotion policies, and labor-intensive growth paths.

In chapter 6, Barbara Stallings, Nancy Birdsall, and Julie Clugage shed new light on the debate on growth and equality by examining the growth-equality relationship within various regions. They argue that the relationship between growth and equality is more likely to be positive where a labor-intensive growth path and rapid accumulation of human and physical capital drive down the scarcity rents to physical and human capital, reducing the skewness of income distribution. This happened in East Asia but not in Latin America. The authors conclude that the "initial" distribution of assets (say, in the early 1960s) was more equitable in East Asia than in Latin America and that this was an important factor in allowing more egalitarian growth in East Asia. The authors note also that resource endowments in Northeast Asia were propitious to the development of labor-intensive production patterns.

Poverty and Inequality in a Rapid-Growth Setting: The Case of Chile

Building upon the theoretical analysis and international comparisons presented in part I of the book, part II, written by senior Chilean government officials, focuses on the case of Chile, an economy that has undergone significant economic transformation along market-oriented lines in the last two decades and has enjoyed since the mid-1980s sustained economic expansion, with annual growth rates of around 7 percent for more than 12 years up to 1997. A main policy concern in the 1990s in Chile, as the country restored democracy after 17 years of military rule, has been making the fruits of growth and modernization accessible to a wider spectrum of the population through a socially oriented market economy. The Chilean case in a way represents an open challenge, still inconclusive, to match market-driven prosperity with social equity.

In chapter 7, Eduardo Aninat discusses the importance of improving income distribution as Chile continues to grow. To this end, he reviews the main elements of Chilean fiscal, macro-, and social policies. He discusses the rationale of Chile's policy of generating positive public savings as one direct public-sector contribution to the overall pool of savings and hence to growth. He also assesses the potential distributive impact of globalization, a cornerstone of the Chilean development experience. Finally, he provides an overview of the educational goals of the Frei administration and reviews the fiscal dimensions of the proposed educational reform program.

In chapter 8, on income distribution and poverty, Kevin Cowan and José De Gregorio examine the growth-equity relationship by providing new data for the case of Chile. The authors discuss several indicators of distribution and present data showing that, in spite of some worsening income distribution in Chile in the early 1990s, poverty has declined, consumption is more evenly distributed, and the quality of life (mostly in the material dimension) has improved. Because short-run changes in income distribution are based much more on cyclical changes—booms and recessions—than on structural factors, these other distribution measures are important in evaluating the outcome of Chilean social policies over the past decade. The authors show that, while the income distribution ratio for Chile (between the top and bottom quintiles) is 13, a high number by international standards, the ratio drops below 9 when government expenditures are included. Also, the percentage point reduction in the poverty rate that results from a one point increase in GDP is increasing in Chile—in other words, growth is becoming more effective at reducing poverty. While income distribution worsened slightly between 1990 and 1994, the authors link this to a downturn in the business cycle instead of attributing it to a negative long-run relationship between growth and equity. Placed in the larger context of this book, the evidence on Chile presented by Cowan and De Gregorio provides support for a positive relationship between growth and poverty reduction, although the study still shows an inconclusive relationship between growth and income distribution. This latter result is disturbing in the sense that, in spite of the fact that GDP has roughly doubled in a decade or so, the way income is distributed is still highly unequal in Chile.

In chapter 9, José Pablo Arellano provides data on the dramatic increases in targeted social spending that occurred over the period 1990–96 in Chile, and the corresponding increases in tax revenues as a percentage of GDP, in order to make the implementation of progressive social policies compatible with a balanced fiscal policy. He presents an overview of the social programs funded during this time period and some indicators of their success in boosting the quality of life of the poor. Arellano argues that there is a choice to be made between permanently providing the poor with monetary subsidies and investing in education and health. He believes that Chile has chosen and will continue to choose the latter, particularly with substantial investments in education. He concurs with Cowan and De Gregorio in cautioning against looking solely at changes in income distribution to denote improvements or declines in social equity since current investments in education will not be reflected in improved income distribution for several years. Arellano believes that improved access to higher quality education and infrastructure is raising the Chilean standard of living, improving both growth and equity.

In chapter 10, Sergio Molina provides an overview of the comprehensive educational reform program now under way in Chile to improve the quantity, quality, and equity of the school system. The main policies oriented toward improving the quantity and quality of education include a planned increase in total school hours, modernization of the curriculum, better equipment and infrastructure, and the creation of a system of "schools of excellence" in populous neighborhoods. This reform is to be financed from several sources, including retention of the value added tax (VAT) at current rates (rather than a planned reduction). Improvements in the quality of education must lead to improvements in equity since it is the poorest children who have been most adversely affected by low-quality schools in populous neighborhoods and rural areas. Other components of the reform include improved and expanded teacher training and modernization and decentralization of the educational administration.

In chapter 11, Jorge Arrate comments on the underpinnings of the labor system and current labor policies in Chile. Chilean labor policy focuses on three goals: boosting worker productivity (including more balanced labor relations, job mobility, and flexibility), training, and humanization of the workplace. Arrate suggests that there is much overlap between the mechanisms used to boost labor productivity and those meant to increase social equity. These include the provision of quality training, maintenance of high employment levels, an unemployment insurance program, better employer-employee relationships and dialogue, and a minimum wage policy. Minister Arrate argues that this set of labor policies is intended to integrate labor into the social market economy.

In chapter 12, former secretary general of the presidency Genaro Arriagada provides an overview of the long-term evolution of social policy in Chile. He explains that from the early 1900s through the early 1970s successive governments gradually moved toward providing near universal access to social services (education, health, housing, pensions) to a wide segment of the population from the poor to the upper middle class, making Chile the Latin American equivalent of a welfare state. This situation changed under the military regime that took power in September 1973. With the structural adjustment measures of the 1970s and 1980s, social spending was reduced and transfers were targeted at the most needy, cutting off the middle class from access to largely subsidized social services. The focus of social policies shifted to a reliance on economic growth to reduce poverty assisted by targeted subsidies and a reduced central government role in the provision of social services. During the Pinochet regime, Arriagada argues, the preoccupation with reducing income and wealth inequalities was viewed as obstructing market mechanisms and unnecessary since economic growth was thought to be the chief mechanism for poverty reduction.

Arriagada explains that in the 1990s, under a democratic government, social policy has moved away from the provision of direct subsidies toward the creation of opportunities for Chileans, particularly the large segment of those who fall between the indigent and the middle class. This is in line with the goal of making the benefits of growth widely shared by various groups in society, matching rapid economic growth with political and social support for these policies. The Frei government still uses transfers in an attempt to meet its goal of eradicating extreme poverty by the year 2000, but the thrust of its social policy is shifting from a focus on assistance to the poor to one of equal opportunity within the context of rapid economic growth. While economic growth is vital to the creation of new opportunities, Arriagada asserts that it is insufficient because it does not alter the distribution of opportunities or the political voice of the marginalized (the rural poor and the urban unemployed or underemployed) and the working classes, nor does it ensure that opportunity will be equally available to all members of society. Current social policy will provide opportunities for all Chileans by endowing them with the tools they need to excel and by putting an end to discrimination against the poor. Strategic areas of intervention discussed in Arriagada's chapter include: augmenting education, improving job quality and productivity, enhancing the quantity and quality of public services for the poor, providing low-income groups with access to an efficient judicial system, fostering business skills among microentrepreneurs, and providing access to quality housing.

Lessons and Challenges

Some of the main lessons, findings, and challenges that emerge from this volume can be summarized as follows:

The traditional view that sees an inherent conflict — or tradeoff — between wealth creation (economic growth) and wealth distribution (social equity) is based on the Kaldoran savings hypothesis and the Kuznets curve. New analytical work and country experiences have challenged this view and identified channels explaining why economic growth and reduced inequality can go together. These mechanisms emphasize: (1) the positive effect on private investment of the reduced social tensions associated with less income and wealth inequality; (2) the potential for greater savings among the poor, who can realize profitable investment opportunities at the household and microenterprise levels; (3) an education-mediated positive correlation between economic growth and social equity; and (4) the positive effects of more equalitarian distribution on aggregate demand, capacity utilization, and investment.

New, more consistent time-series data for a wide range of countries has challenged the Kuznets curve's inverted U-shaped relation between inequality and per capita income levels. The new evidence shows that growth is a central ingredient for poverty reduction; in turn, this evidence is ambiguous on the relationship between growth and income distribution. Economic growth per se is unlikely to improve income distribution.

A renewed interest in the theory of distributive justice is emerging. New developments in this area highlight the role of background factors such as initial wealth, talent, gender, and family status, which are often beyond an individual's control but are important in generating social inequality vis-à-vis elements pertaining to the realm of individual responsibility such as work effort, ambition, risk taking, and entrepreneurial capacity. The ethical implications of each set of factors in assessing the justice of a given distribution of wealth and income are very different. By highlighting the role of "circumstances" and predetermined individual and social factors, this new literature on distributive justice provides some justification for treating inequality as a central concern of public policy.

At the policy level, this volume identifies the role of providing equal access to wealth-creating assets like credit, land, education, and health (mainly to the poor) as crucial to fostering economic growth, social equity, and upward mobility in society. The educational reform launched in Chile in the mid-1990s is an important experiment in seeking efficiency and distributive justice through an improved educational system. Social safety nets, targeted subsidies, and maintenance of a basic food level are also crucial to the support of vulnerable groups and the protection of low-income groups at time of negative shocks, downturns, and/or recessions. Redistribution of assets like land and democratization of the ownership of the national capital stock constitute progressive social policies that deserve more attention by policymakers.

Fiscal policy must balance its capacity to devise adequate social spending programs with its ability to increase tax revenues. The experience of Chile in the 1990s is an interesting attempt at combining social programs meant to improve the conditions of the poor with fiscal surpluses in the budget. Macroeconomic stability and political feasibility provide the boundaries for the sustainability of progressive social policy. A balance between meeting social objectives and respect for macro- and political realities is essential to sensible social policy-making. To be sustained, social policies need the political backing of the beneficiaries voiced through their social organizations and political representatives.

The Chilean experience of the 1990s is a case study of the search for a durable marriage between rapid economic growth and social equity. Rapid growth, associated with macrostability, global integration, private sector–led investment, and political stability, has been very important in reducing poverty in Chile; however, the distribution of income remains unequal despite more than a decade of rapid economic expansion and the restoration of democracy. In Chile, the reduction of inequality remains as a pending objective for the twenty-first century.

NOTE

1. Kaldor (1957) assumed that a high proportion of profits and a low proportion of wages are saved.

REFERENCES

Kaldor, N. 1957. "A Model of Economic Growth." *Economic Journal* 67:591–624.

Marx, K. 1970. "Critique of the Gotha Program." In K. Marx and F. Engels, *Selected Works.* London: Lawrence and Wishart.

Polyani, K. 1957. *The Great Transformation: The Political and Economic Origins of Our Time.* Boston: Beacon Press.

Roemer, J. 1996. *Theories of Distributive Justice.* Cambridge, MA: Harvard University Press.

Roemer, J. 1998. *Equality of Opportunity.* Cambridge, MA: Harvard University Press.

Solimano, Andrés, ed. 1998. *Social Inequality: Values, Growth, and the State.* Ann Arbor: University of Michigan Press.

PART I

Equity, Growth, and Development

Theory and International Evidence

CHAPTER 2

Beyond Unequal Development: An Overview

Andrés Solimano

In the 1940s, 1950s, and 1960s, development theory emphasized market failures, discontinuities, irreversibilities, and excessive social inequality. The dominant development paradigm stressed the need for the state to create an adequate physical infrastructure and the institutional and social conditions required for development. This would entail implementing large-scale public investment programs, planning, and policies aimed at social modernization in the areas of education, health, social protection, and housing.

In the 1980s and 1990s, this paradigm changed. In a way, development problems were reduced to growth problems, and the lack of sustained growth, particularly in the 1980s in Latin America, was thought to have resulted from state interference in the market process, both internationally through trade protection and nationally through the over-regulation of goods, capital, and labor markets, and extended state ownership of national productive assets.

Economic growth (material progress) became the main development goal in the policies known as the Washington Consensus. Growth was to be supported by (1) macroeconomic stabilization — understood basically as the reduction of inflation and fiscal deficits — and (2) structural reforms such as trade liberalization, financial deregulation, privatization, and a decisive shift to a smaller state role in the economy.

Previous concerns with reducing inequalities of income and wealth were eschewed in favor of an agenda dominated by macrostabilization and liberalization. The experience of the 1990s is showing that the combination of fiscal adjustment and market liberalization, although necessary policy steps to reduce macroimbalances and increase efficiency, is insufficient to bring about stable and equitable development. Reality is showing several difficulties in the adjustment and development process that were underestimated by the policies of the Washington Consensus: (1) the transition from low inflation to sustained growth and development is often long; (2) the excessive emphasis on fiscal adjustment neglected the risks of premature financial liberalization; (3) globalization has

17

increased the frequency, scope, and severity of financial and macrocrises; (4) governance problems have been reflected in corruption, dysfunctional institutions, and social conflict; (5) poverty is persistent and positively correlated with macrocrises; and (6) inequalities of income and wealth, both across and within countries, seem to have increased in the last decade in Latin America.

Addressing these issues may call for a rethinking of existing development paradigms. This chapter focuses on one important dimension of the development process — namely, inequality — and asks how we can move beyond the trap of unequal development. For that purpose, this chapter selectively reviews two strands of literature pertaining to our subject: (1) recent developments in distributive justice that provide an interphase between the political philosophy of justice and the economics of income distribution and social welfare; and (2) the analytics and empirics of the relationship between inequality and growth. The underlying idea is that more egalitarian development is feasible and desirable and that positive complementarity can be found between distributive justice, social equity, and economic development.

Then this chapter turns to social policies. The discussion continues by identifying policies compatible with both rapid growth and more egalitarian development: structural social policies, emergency social safety nets, and policies intended to foster egalitarian access to wealth-creation processes and assets (e.g., education, credit, and ownership of productive assets). The scope and limits of targeting, trickle-down growth, and the private provision of social services are also reassessed in their role as foundations for social policies behind the Washington Consensus.

Poverty and Inequality: What Do We Mean by Social Equity?

A minimalist approach views the reduction of absolute poverty as the only valid concern of social policy. Public policy must assure that most (ideally all) of the population is above the poverty line and that no vulnerable groups (the elderly, children, the disabled) suffer income deprivation. As society reaches a threshold of basic needs satisfied for the population as a whole, according to this view, subsequent inequalities can be considered largely irrelevant. The extent to which the reduction of social inequality is a valid additional policy objective is a complex issue related to at least two considerations: (1) ethical and moral questions of distributive justice; and (2) the impact of income inequality on other policy objectives such as sustained economic growth, overall development, sociopolitical balance, and the ability to conduct public policy.

The Theory of Distributive Justice

The theory of distributive justice[1] focuses on the causes of inequality and provides useful philosophical and economic foundations for a discussion of inequality.

Outside Factors and Personal Responsibility

If observed income and wealth inequality reflects, to a large extent, differences in initial endowments of wealth, talent, family connections, race, or gender — factors mostly beyond the control of the individual or (in philosophical terms) a set of "morally arbitrary" factors — then inequality becomes an ethical issue, as key wealth-creating factors are beyond the control of the individual. However, observed inequality of income, wealth, or consumption can and do also reflect individual differences in effort, ambition, and risk taking. To the extent that these elements reflect personal preferences and belong to the realm of "individual responsibility," they do not necessarily constitute an ethical problem from the viewpoint of the theory of distributive justice. This provides an attractive framework for distinguishing between equality of outcomes (e.g., income or wealth) and equality of opportunities, a subject we will deal with later. This sharp separation between arbitrary and nonarbitrary factors is blurred when it is recognized that "morally arbitrary" factors (e.g., initial wealth and talents) are likely to be related to the formation of preferences and the concept of individual responsibility, two elements that ultimately influence effort levels and the willingness to take risks. In fact, one may think that the perception of a wealthy individual of what constitutes "success in life" (or acceptable levels of welfare) can be very different for the rich than for the poor. This circularity between resources and preferences, or between "morally arbitrary factors" and "personal responsibility," makes the theme of social inequality both exciting and overly complex.

Alternative Views

The fundamentally different visions of society found among various schools of thought affect views on inequality.[2] Liberalism, neo-Marxism, and libertarianism are three main schools of thought in this regard. Liberals such as Rawls emphasize that initial wealth, family background, social connections, and the like can be unfairly distributed at the "birth lottery." For Rawls, the organization of a just society requires a social contract negotiated under a "veil of ignorance" with regard to the distribution of wealth and other traits that shape individuals' interests in society. The idea is that a fair social contract must be independent of background conditions; otherwise, the rules of the game will be biased in favor of the wealthy. For Rawls, a social arrangement is just only if it primarily benefits those who are worst off in society. This is called the difference principle.[3]

Utilitarianism and welfare economics provide another analytical base for liberalism, different from the social contractualism of Locke and Rawls. In contrast to Rawls, utilitarians avoid judging the justice of a given distribution of income and wealth in society. They focus only on maximizing total personal utility, regardless of how the benefits are distributed among different members of society. Moreover, welfare economics sees distributive outcomes as the result of voluntary wealth accumulation over generations, with the remuneration of factors of production given by productivity and effort levels. The lack of attention to issues of distributive justice by utilitarianism is in contrast to the emphasis placed on features (background factors) outside the individual's control and responsibility stressed by Rawls and the theory of distributive justice.

Another perspective is provided by neo-Marxism. In particular, Marxist economics sees unequal property relations and the command of productive wealth in capitalism as the main factors generating and reproducing inequalities over time.[4] Neo-Marxism eschews the idea of a social contract negotiated under the veil of ignorance. On the contrary, it stresses that the owners of productive wealth design or influence institutions that are beneficial to their own interests: hence, the neo-Marxist claim of the unfair nature of capitalist society. In contrast, libertarians such as Robert Nozick see the possession of wealth and the right to enjoy its benefits as natural rights of the individual, a part of the "self-ownership" that includes the right to private use of productive assets and natural resources.[5] Libertarians propose a "minimal state" devoid of the powers of taxation that expropriate the fruits of individual effort and risk taking.

Concepts of Equality

An important issue relates to the concept of equality.[6] A crucial distinction has been made between equality of opportunity and equality of outcome. As mentioned, a person is not responsible for the set of opportunities he (or she) faces at birth: race, gender, talent, wealth, and family background. However, the individual is responsible for transforming favorable opportunities into positive outcomes. Equality of access to wealth-creating factors such as education or credit is termed the equality of opportunity. This is a valid policy objective from the viewpoint of distributive justice. In contrast, making equality of outcome, measured by income or wealth, the goal of distributive justice could be problematic provided that outcomes depend to a considerable extent on voluntary choices by individuals regarding effort put in the workplace in the case of workers and/or risk-taking attitudes in the case of people undertaking entrepreneurial activities (see table 2.1).

Making equality of opportunity the only valid criteria for social policy circumvents the fact that effort and risk taking are not fully independent of initial background conditions. A more "activist" view of equality would qualify the equality of opportunity and expand the concept in several directions. First, it would distinguish between formal and effective equality of opportunity (e.g., education might be a universal right in a country, but its effective access may depend on the income level of the student). Second, it would call for compensation of those relatively less lucky in the "birth lottery." The implementation of compensation schemes will entail policies of income transfer, affirmative action, and others that go beyond pursuing only equality of opportunity and equalize access to education but do not compensate for other background conditions that are important for an individual's success in life.[7]

Inequality, Growth, and Development: Complementarities and Tradeoffs[8]

Let's move from the (complicated) questions of distributive justice to the macrointeractions (tradeoffs and/or complementarities) between inequality, economic growth, and long-run development. Is income and wealth inequality the price to be paid for accelerated economic growth? Or, conversely, does inequality retard economic growth? How does inequality evolve during the course of economic development? These key questions need to be addressed.

TABLE 2.1. Determinants of Income/Wealth and Concepts of Equality

Determinants of Income and Wealth (the concept of equality)	Initial Assets, Talent, Gender, Race, Family Status ("outside" factors)	Effort Levels, Risk Taking, Entrepreneurial Capacities (personal responsibility)
Equality of opportunity	X (Main Focus)	
Equality of outcomes	X (Main Focus)	X (Main Focus)

Growth and Inequality Links

The relationship between economic growth and social inequality at the macrolevel depends on how the growth process is specified.[9] In models of savings-driven growth, if profit recipients save in greater proportion than wage earners do (linear saving functions), a pattern of income distribution concentrated on capital will increase national savings and accelerate the rate of economic growth (all of what is saved is invested; see table 2.2). This model supports the "conservative" notion that a more equitable distribution of income retards economic growth through a negative effect on the national savings ratio; it points, then, to the existence of a tradeoff between growth and equity.

Conversely, neo-Keynesian and endogenous growth theories view growth mainly as an investment-driven process and emphasize complementarities between growth and social equality. In neo-Keynesian models in which aggregate demand plays a role in the determination of long-run growth, income distribution affects growth through both effective demand (consumption, investment demand, exports) and the rate of creation of new productive capacity.

Redistribution of income to wage earners can increase aggregate demand and growth in the short term provided that positive consumption effects outweigh adverse investment and export effects. However, the initial increase in aggregate demand will trigger supply constraints, generating inflationary and balance of payments disequilibria that will limit or simply reverse the initial income redistribution.[10] In the endogenous growth literature, countries with large personal income and wealth inequalities invite, through a political mechanism, higher taxation and the adoption of redistributive policies that depress the profitability of capital, hampering investment and slowing output growth. The main implication here is that initial inequality is bad for subsequent growth. Other channels have also been highlighted to show a negative correlation between personal income inequality and economic growth, wealth, and income: inequality can lead to sociopolitical instability and/or populist economic policies that are ultimately destabilizing and hamper private capital formation and economic growth. The new literature combines investment-driven growth with a political mechanism transmitting public preferences for pro-growth versus pro-redistribution policies into actual government policies. The political mechanisms range from elections or referendums to social pressure (social activism, strikes, and so on). The causality goes from initial inequality to future growth. Interestingly, this literature carries a "progressive" message that social inequality is bad for growth, although it identifies redistributive policies (particularly those

TABLE 2.2

Models/Theories	Model Closure		Economic Mechanism		Sociopolitical Mechanism		Causality		Type of Relationship Inequality/Growth	
	Saving-Driven Growth	Investment-Driven Growth	Classic Saving Function	Profitability and Investment	Median Voter	Bargaining Power of Capitalist Workers	Income Distribution	Growth to Income Distribution	Inverse	Direct
Classic	X		X				X			X
Solow	X							X		X
Kaldor		X	X					X		X
New growth theory/ endogenous policy		X		X	X		X		X	
Wage-led and profit-led growth theories		X		X		X	X		?	
Neo-Marxist theories										
(a) Long-run	X		X			X	X			X
(b) Profit squeeze/social structures of accumulation		X		X		X	X			X

Source: Solimano 1998, 56.

that hamper investment) as the reason why initial inequality leads to slower growth.

Empirical Evidence

The methodology of this inequality-growth literature is largely dominated by cross-sectional or panel regression analysis.[11] Several empirical studies tend to support the hypothesis that inequality (an explanatory variable) has a negative, often statistically significant, effect on the rate of output growth (the dependent variable in the regressions) after controlling for variables such as initial per capita income, levels of education, and political participation. This result seems to hold for separate samples of developed and less developed economies (see Persson and Tabellini 1992) and is robust with regard to alternative functional forms of the distribution-growth relationship and different measures of inequality (share of top quintile, Gini coefficient, Theil coefficient; see Clarke 1992). However, not all studies agree on this. For example, Fishlow (1995) shows that the negative correlation between inequality and growth fails to be detected when a dummy for Latin America, a region with high inequality, is included in the regressions. The influence of the political regime (democracy or nondemocracy) on the inequality and growth nexus seems less sure. While Persson and Tabellini (1992) found that the negative relationship between inequality and growth holds only for democracies, Clarke (1992) and Alesina and Rodrik (1994) found no significant impact of the political regime on the sign and significance of the distribution parameter in growth regressions. It is worth mentioning that all the models tested, including the economic and political mechanisms, are reduced forms. A structural test of the political mechanism (median voter) proposed in the theory is hard to find.

A recent World Bank study by Deininger and Squire (1995b) shows that most of the recent tests of the negative relationship between initial inequality and subsequent economic growth are based on income distribution data of limited coverage and with little cross-country or temporal comparability. Moreover, the results obtained in previous studies have to be carefully interpreted, as they are estimates drawn from reduced forms of a structural model in which other variables may determine the joint comovement of growth and income distribution observed in the data. Moreover, in a related study Liu, Squire, and Zou (1995) use recent and more consistent data on income distribution to show that income inequality is relatively stable within countries and over time, in stark contrast to the behavior of the rates of growth GDP, which do change rapidly and are characterized by very low persistence.

These two studies strongly question the accuracy of the empirical tests of the new growth theory on income inequality.

Inequality and Development Links: The Kuznets Curve

The relationship between development levels (proxied by the level of per capita income and income) and inequality (measured by the Gini coefficients or the share between top and bottom quintiles or deciles) postulated by Simon Kuznets has been subject to controversy and empirical testing for a long time. As is well known, the Kuznets hypothesis posits the existence of a nonlinear relationship between per capita income and an index of income inequality, reflected in an inverted U-shaped curve; income inequality worsens in the initial stages of development, characterized by low per capita income levels, and improves thereafter as income per person rises. The Kuznets mechanisms focus on the shift from a surplus-labor agricultural sector paying subsistence wages to a modern industrial sector with higher wages during the initial stages of development. Later, inequality declines due to a narrowing of wage differentials as the pool of labor surplus is exhausted and the skills profile of the work force is upgraded through formal education and learning by doing during the course of development. The causality in Kuznets goes from development levels to inequality, and the sign of the relationship evolves over historical time.

Empirical Evidence

The Kuznets curve spurred a vast empirical effort devoted to testing its shape, determining its robustness with regard to the selection of countries and time periods, and detecting the turning points at which income distribution begins to improve.

The empirical cross-sectional work of Ahluwalia (1976), Lindert and Williamson (1985), Adelman and Robinson (1989), Bourguignon and Morrisson (1990), and others tends to give (qualified) support to the existence of the Kuznets curve. In addition, for cross-country regressions the inequality portion of the Kuznets curve tends to be more unstable than the portion of declining inequality (see fig. 2.1). Since the inequality part of the curve comprises countries in a range of lower to moderate per capita income levels, the relationship is more unstable for these countries.[12] In contrast, it seems to be more established that inequality tends to decline for countries at the intermediate and higher levels of per capita income (see fig. 2.2).[13] However, studies of individual countries in Latin America (Colombia, Brazil, Argentina) and of

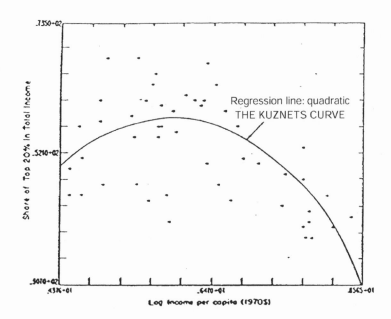

Fig. 2.1. The Kuznets curve: international 60 country cross section from the 1960s and 1970s. (From Ahluwalia 1976, table 8, 340–41.)

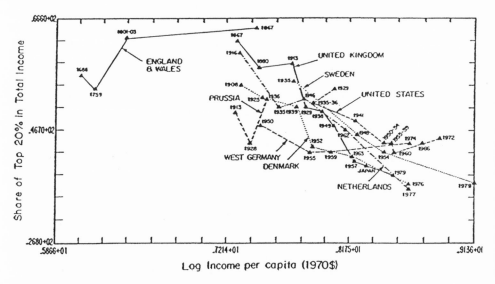

Fig. 2.2. The Kuznets curve: historical time series from five European countries and America. (Reproduced from Lindert and Williamson 1985.)

Asian countries are reported to conform to the Kuznets curve pattern (see Fields and Jakubson 1993). A comparison of the impact of inequality on growth between Latin America and East Asia is conducted in Birdsall and Sabot (1994).

Two World Bank studies (Deininger and Squire 1995a, 1995b) have produced an expanded data base with improved coverage and consistency on income distribution to reevaluate existing studies of the Kuznets curve. These studies, by pooling cross-sectional with time-series data, show that the Kuznets curve holds only for a very small set of countries (10 percent of the sample) and that in general no statistically significant relationship between levels of income and inequality is found for more than 75 percent of the sample. The "universal Kuznets curve" was not detected in the data. These studies cast doubt on the existence and robustness of the Kuznets curve. More research is needed to reconcile the new World Bank and previous evidence on the Kuznets curve. In any case, it appears that as countries move up the per capita income ladder inequality tends to decline. Important practical questions, then, are at what levels of per capita income inequality starts declining and how public policies can help accelerate this process.

Policy Issues

Growth and Equality: Are They Compatible?

A central policy question is whether public policies oriented toward improving income distribution are compatible with high and sustained growth? The macrogrowth models reviewed here offer arguments to support "conservative" views that redistribution deters growth as well as "progressive" views in which redistribution and growth are compatible, and even mutually reinforcing, complementary policy goals. Analytically, the conservative view finds support in two models. In a full-capacity, growing economy, income redistribution to relatively low-savings groups can depress the aggregate savings ratio, leading to a decline in growth. In investment-driven models, redistributive policies that entail higher taxation and/or regulation depress privately appropriated returns on human capital and physical investment and harm growth.

Are we thus condemned to accept social inequality as the price of high growth policies? Is "conservative equilibrium" inescapable? Not necessarily. Three arguments are in order here. First, the message of the Kuznets curve is that the growth process itself is "equalizing" beyond a certain threshold of per capita income (the turning point of the curve), making the fruits of progress and development available to a greater portion of the population. Second, beyond trickle down, policy intervention to assure broad social access to education (and credit) can have a big payoff. Market equilibrium can yield substantial underinvestment, particularly in human capital, for those at the bottom of the income distribution ladder who cannot pay for their education and face very limited access to capital markets. The rewards, in terms of accelerated growth, of education widening are bound to be sizable. Third, a more equitable distribution of income and economic opportunities also contributes to social peace and political stability, key ingredients in a policy framework conducive to investment, innovation, and growth. Ultimately, social equity and economic growth can go hand with hand if properly articulated so as to respect some key binding economic and political constraints in society.

Social Policies and the Washington Consensus: Scope and Limits

In line with market-based economic reform, during the last decade countries have moved away from traditional social policies that often involved across the board subsidies (to large segments of the population) of basic foodstuffs, public utilities such as water and electricity, and universal access to education and health services. For a while in many countries, these policies resulted in a considerable reduction in analphabetism, substantial educational upgrading of the middle class and lower income groups, and improvement in health indicators. However, these policies eventually led to a growing fiscal burden, and they often primarily benefited higher income groups. The social policies implicit in the Washington Consensus (in fact, this consensus has been criticized for its lack of explicit social policies; see Stiglitz 1998), which are tailored to a market-based policy framework, rest on the following principles:

> Economic growth should be the main engine for poverty reduction and improvements in living standards (the "trickle-down" effect).
> Relative prices and the market mechanism must guide resource allocation and the incentives to save and invest. Social policies must avoid affecting the relative price structure of the economy through subsidies and indirect taxation. Price controls of basic foodstuffs must be eliminated. Marginal cost pricing must dictate user fees for public utilities.
> Social policies must be explicitly focused on — or targeted to — the most vulnerable segments of the population (the elderly, children, the disabled) and the poorest groups in society (rural popu-

lations, workers in the informal sector, urban families in extreme poverty).

Private sector participation in the provision and management of basic social services such as education and health must be encouraged through privatization and/or concession schemes.

The explicit objective of social policy is poverty reduction. Correcting large income or wealth inequalities is not an explicit policy objective.

Although a full evaluation of the implementation and results of social policies based on these principles is beyond the scope of this chapter, a few observations are in order.

As mentioned above, *economic growth* is seen as the main vehicle for poverty reduction and the improvement of living standards. There is no question that economic growth is very important. Growth directly generates employment and real income for labor market participants and provides — through tax receipts — fiscal revenues to the state that can be used to finance social policies. Moreover, a growing economy is bound to ease distributional conflict as competing claims are over a "growing pie" rather than constituting a zero-sum game. However, economic growth also has limitations as a mechanism to enable poverty reduction and the improvement of living standards. First, the potential of growth for poverty reduction depends not only on the level of growth but on its composition: it has to be labor intensive and must benefit unskilled labor. The spatial (or regional) composition of production must favor poorer regions more than others. Second, GDP, or any aggregate output measure, is a yardstick that omits distributive considerations.[14] Third, output growth does not directly reach vulnerable groups such as the elderly, children, the disabled, subsistence farmers, and those outside the labor market. Fourth, GDP statistics often underreport informal sector activities in which lower income groups are involved. Family- or public-based redistribution is needed to reach these segments. Fifth, GDP is a commodity- or "wealth-based" measure of economic welfare that does not include nonmarket benefits (such as political freedom or the psychological value of belonging to a community) and detriments (environmental degradation, crime, or urban congestion). Sixth, unlike traditional social policies, which have a political constituency in the urban working class, the strong unions of the middle class (teachers, doctors), and other interest groups, the new social policies have as beneficiaries poor and vulnerable groups with a weak voice and feeble political organizations. This creates tenuous political incentives for active poverty reduction beyond that provided by economic growth and may be an important factor in chronic poverty.

Another piece of the new strategy of social policy is targeting. The emphasis on precisely defining beneficiary groups is a reaction to social policies that often reached, at a high cost, the middle class and the rich. A basic principle of targeting is to focus social policy on the poor while avoiding the nonpoor.[15] In this context, targeting is more effective in terms of reaching the "real" poor, and at a substantially reduced cost, than untargeted, broad-based, social policy.

However, targeting is not problem free, either. First, targeting makes the beneficiary a passive "victim" rather than an active agent with policy responses and choices.[16] Second, the informational and incentive problems are serious. Delimiting the beneficiaries and their poverty features is not easy (e.g., an information problem). The ability of the state to reach the most vulnerable groups cannot be taken for granted. Moreover, some targeted groups have a more active political voice than others, biasing the transfer of resources to them (e.g., an incentive problem). Political favoritism and clientelism among certain groups can lead to a failure to reach the most needy.

Private sector provision and delivery of social services such as education and health care are another component of a market-based approach to social policy. Private sector involvement in social sectors can help release the financial and human resources of the state, allowing it to focus its efforts on lower income groups. Privatization of social services seems to work well for the adequate provision — in terms of quantity and quality — of education and health services for high-income and the upper-middle-class segments that can afford to pay for such services. However, for low-income groups and other segments of the middle class the situation is different. As their ability to pay is low, they depend on demand subsidies — for example, a voucher system — for access to high-cost, privately provided social services or else they have to be served by the state. In addition, in the case of private health systems, providers often have clauses that exclude the elderly, the chronically ill, and those with large families from access to these programs, precisely the groups that need the most protection.

The coexistence of relatively poor, state-provided education and health systems along with modern, affluent, private systems creates serious incentives and equity problems. Schoolteachers, university professors, physicians, and paramedics often have considerable incentives to work in the highly paid private sector, decapitalizing the state sector. Moreover, while some citizens will have access to first-class education and health services, others will face the impoverished education and health services provided by the state. A main challenge is how to guarantee good quality, cost efficient, social services for the large segments of the population that cannot afford to pay for the services delivered in the private system and therefore have to be served by the state.

Policies to Match Growth, Social Equity, and Poverty Reduction

Policies oriented toward increasing individual productivity and earning capacities are crucial to matching economic growth with better income distribution and less poverty. Education is a clear-cut case; it endows people with greater human capital and promotes social mobility.

The quality of education and the extent to which the poor have access to it matter also. However, education is a supply-side policy, which, to be effective, requires a corresponding level of demand for human resources, which in turn depends on the level of effective demand and the pace of growth. A bad equilibrium has pools of educated and well-qualified people who are un- or underemployed. Health-related policies are also essential for building up human capital. An improvement in health capacities reduces vulnerability and boosts the quality of life. Broadening and democratizing access to credit also provide an equalizing, productivity-enhancing mechanism, as many latent projects identified and developed by small-scale entrepreneurs and households fail due to lack of credit and financing. Policies of asset distribution regarding land reform and broad-based ownership of productive capital — say, following privatization — are also worth considering.

The recent literature claiming that "inequality harms growth" stresses that redistributive policies penalize private investment and growth. This calls attention to the way redistribution is carried out. Capital taxation can depress profit rates and lead to lower investment; the level of taxation has to be monitored, as high taxation invites evasion besides hampering savings, investment, and growth. However, investment is also very sensitive to uncertainty and sociopolitical instability. From that perspective, policies oriented toward reducing large social inequalities can have a significant "social-peace dividend," which is essential to fostering a framework conducive to investment and growth.

The promotion of economic growth as a basic engine for achieving better living standards and poverty reduction has to be not only maintained but complemented with a greater awareness of the limits of commodity-based welfare. A healthy physical environment, economic and physical security, civic participation, and political freedom are all very important dimensions of meaningful human self-realization beyond the consumption of goods and services.

In addition, paternalistic social policies have to be avoided. This is a defect of both traditional social policies, with their broad-based subsidization, and targeting, with its passive approach of unreactive beneficiaries. The web of community and nongovernmental organizations that has appeared in recent years in many countries forms a useful bridge between individual atomization and the state (with its limited administrative and financial capacities). These intermediate organizations can and do play an important role in the design and management of social policy.

Private provision of some social services can serve a useful role among higher income groups. It can be also a source of innovation that can permeate the state-based provision of social services. In developing countries, it is clear that the vast majority of the population needs access to either subsidized or state-provided education and health services. How the two systems can coexist and how to improve the quality of the services provided by the state are important open questions.

Finally, most of these policies can be viewed as the "structural social policies" envisaged in the framework of a growing economy. The situation is different when a macroeconomic crisis leads to higher unemployment and a decline in real wages and income, particularly for the poor and vulnerable. In this case, social safety nets are needed. The institutional and financial requirements of solving emergency social problems are often less burdensome than those of structural social policies. Social safety nets often involve the provision of emergency employment to those who lose jobs after fiscal retrenchment, the delivery of food and medicine to children in schools, and guaranteed minimum income support.

Concluding Remarks

Some of the main topics and conclusions of this chapter can be summarized as follows:

Social policies in developing countries in the last decade or so have been defined almost exclusively in terms of poverty reduction. A fresh look at the issue of income distribution and the reduction of social inequality as valid policy targets is needed.

The modern theory of distributive justice distinguishes between "outside" (or morally arbitrary) factors (gender, race, initial assets, talent) and "personal responsibility" elements (effort, risk-taking attitudes) in shaping the level of income, wealth, and welfare of the individual in society. Social inequality is a reflection of individual differences in these two sets of wealth-creating factors.

Any meaningful social policy needs a definition of *equality*. Equality of opportunity (e.g., to education or bank credit), if it is to be effective rather than formal, needs some complementary action. Additional concepts such as equality of outcome calls for compensating mechanisms for poor endowments of useful traits (e.g., talent, gender) acquired in the "birth lottery."

The new theories of endogenous growth stress the existence of complementarity between social equity and growth. Provided that inequality engenders social conflict, invites taxation of physical investments, and induces economic populism, we can conclude that social inequality hampers economic growth. The empirical evidence based on time series and cross sections seems to support, with some qualifications, the adverse effect of inequality on growth.

The Kuznets curve, which links development levels and income distribution, suggests a trend toward less inequality after "intermediate" levels of per capita income have been reached. Assuming that the Kuznets curve holds, something in dispute now, it is important to discover the plausible levels of per capita income for which a decline in inequality is to be expected and the mechanisms that can bring about that decline.

The "Washington Consensus" has supported social policies that rely on three main pillars: growth-led poverty reduction, targeting, and private sector participation in the delivery of social services. Some loose ends of this strategy are: (1) biased growth patterns in favor of skilled labor and nonlabor factors of production; (2) exclusion of vulnerable groups that do not derive income from the market process; (3) excessive reliance on commodity-based growth for human development, which encompasses also environmental considerations, civic participation in public decision making, and grassroots democracy; (4) political manipulation of beneficiaries and weak institutional capacities to reach targeted groups; and (5) excessive differences in the quality of the social services provided by the private sector and received by high-income groups (and the upper middle class) compared to the modest or poor quality of social services delivered by the state and received by low-income groups.

A catalog of structural social policies oriented toward promoting equitable development must include the provision of broad-based, good quality education and health services; broader access to credit by low-income households and small-scale producers; and egalitarian access to land and ownership of capital stock (say, after privatization).

Social safety nets are needed in periods of macroeconomic crisis that lead to high unemployment, cuts in real wages, and a decline in the real income of the poor. Social safety nets may include policies such as emergency employment programs, food distribution to children and vulnerable groups, and schemes of minimum income support. Austerity programs without social safety nets impose undue costs on the poor, the vulnerable, and the politically weak, making fiscal retrenchment difficult to implement and socially regressive.

NOTES

The comments of Louis Emmerij and Mario Gutierrez on an early version of this essay are appreciated.

1. For a treatment and review of the theory of distributive justice, see Roemer 1996 and Solimano 1998.

2. See Solimano 1998, chap. 2.

3. See Rawls 1971.

4. Marx 1970.

5. Cohen 1995.

6. An influential discussion on this subject in philosophical economics can be found in Dworkin 1981.

7. A full discussion of these issues can be found in Roemer 1998.

8. This section draws on Solimano 1998, chaps. 1, 4.

9. See Solimano 1996.

10. This was the case with the redistributive policies pursued by Allende in Chile in the early 1970s, in Nicaragua in the early 1980s, and in Peru in the mid-1980s.

11. It is still hard to find time-series, historically oriented studies of distribution and growth in this literature.

12. Fields and Jakubson (1993) find a reversal of the Kuznets curve using a "fixed effects" model that allows different countries to lie on Kuznets curves with the same shape but different intercepts. However, in pooled models the standard Kuznets curve is maintained.

13. This does not rule out changes in the levels of inequality even in high per capita income countries as the result of changes in economic policies. This seems to have been the case for the United States under President Reagan and the United Kingdom under Prime Minister Thatcher, when inequality increased (see Krugman 1994).

14. See Sen 1987 and Anand and Sen 1996.

15. See Cornia and Stewart 1996 for an interesting discussion of two types of "errors" in targeting, the E-error (excessive coverage, e.g., reaching the nonpoor) and the F-error (failure to reach to poor).

16. See Anand and Sen 1996.

REFERENCES

Adelman, I., and S. Robinson. 1989. "Income Distribution in Development." In H. Chenery and T. N. Srinivasan, eds., *Handbook of Development Economics.* Vol. 2. North-Holland: Elsevier Science Publishers.

Ahluwalia, M. 1976. "Inequality, Poverty, and Development." *Journal of Development Economics* 3:307–42.

Alesina, A., and D. Rodrik. 1994. "Distributive Politics and Economic Growth." *Quarterly Journal of Economics* 109, no. 2:456–90.

Anand, S., and A. Sen. 1996. "Sustainable Human Development: Concepts and Priorities." Discussion Papers, no. 1. New York: UNDP.

Birdsall, N., and R. Sabot. 1994. "Inequality as a Constraint on Growth in Latin America." IDB. Mimeo.

Bourguignon, F., and C. Morrison. 1990. "Income Distribution, Development, and Foreign Trade: A Cross Section Analysis." *European Economic Review* 34:1113–32.

Clarke, G. 1992. "More Evidence on Income Distribution and Growth." Working Papers, no. 1,064. World Bank.

Cohen, G. A. 1995. *Self-Ownership, Freedom, and Equality.* Cambridge: Cambridge University Press.

Cornia, G., and F. Stewart. 1996. "Two Errors of Targeting." In D. Van de Walle and K. Nead, eds., *Public Spending and the Poor: Theory and Evidence.* Baltimore and London: Johns Hopkins University Press.

Deininger, K., and L. Squire. 1995a. "Measuring Income Inequality: A New Data-Base." World Bank. Mimeo.

———. 1995b. "Inequality and Growth: Results from a New Data-Base." World Bank. Mimeo.

Dworkin, R. 1981. "What Is Equality?" Part 1: "Equality of Welfare"; Part 2: "Equality of Resources." *Philosophy and Public Affairs* 10:185–246, 283–345.

Fields, G., and G. Jakubson. 1993. "New Evidence on the Kuznets Curve." Cornell University. Mimeo.

Fishlow A. 1995. "Inequality, Poverty, and Growth: Where Do We Stand?" In M. Bruno and B. Pleskovic, eds. *Annual World Bank Conference on Development Economics.* Washington, DC: World Bank.

Krugman, P. 1994. *Peddling Prosperity.* New York: Norton.

Lindert, P. H., and J. Williamson. 1985. "Growth, Equality, and History." *Explorations in Economic History* 22:341–77.

Liu H., L. Squire, and H. Zou. 1995. "Explaining International and Intertemporal Variations in Income Inequality." World Bank. Mimeo.

Marx, K. 1970. "Critique of the Gotha Programme." In K. Marx and F. Engels, *Selected Works.* London: Lawrence and Wishart.

Persson, T., and G. Tabellini. 1992. "Growth, Distribution, and Politics." *European Economic Review* 36:593–602.

Rawls, J. 1971. *A Theory of Justice.* Cambridge: Harvard University Press.

Roemer, J. 1996. *Theories of Distributive Justice.* Cambridge: Harvard University Press.

——. 1998. *Equality of Opportunity.* Cambridge: Harvard University Press.

Sen, A. 1987. *The Standard of Living.* Cambridge: Cambridge University Press.

Solimano, A., ed. 1996. *Road Maps to Prosperity: Essays on Growth and Development.* Ann Arbor: University of Michigan Press.

——, ed. 1998. *Social Inequality: Values, Growth, and the State.* Ann Arbor: University of Michigan Press.

Stiglitz, J. 1998. "More Instruments and Broader Goals: Moving toward the Post–Washington Consensus." WIDER Lecture, Helsinki, Finland.

CHAPTER 3

Equity and Growth in Developing Countries: Old and New Perspectives on the Policy Issues

Michael Bruno, Martin Ravallion, and Lyn Squire

Do the poor lose, either absolutely or relatively, from policies that promote aggregate economic growth? Does the answer differ between middle-income newly industrialized economies and low-income developing countries? These questions are not new and were very much at the center of the development debate some 20 years ago in the discussion of how to achieve redistribution with growth (Chenery et al. 1974). They have recently achieved renewed prominence as many countries adjust from the growth crises of the past two decades and as others switch from centrally planned systems to market-based ones. The claim has been made that growth-oriented reform policies of the kind usually advocated by international financial institutions (IFIs) have worsened the lot of the poor.

We begin by reviewing recent evidence indicating that, although income inequality differs significantly across countries, there is no discernable systematic impact over time of growth on inequality. There are exceptions, but generally sustainable economic growth benefits all layers of society, and the gain is roughly in proportion to the initial level of living. Based on the evidence of the past three decades, there seems to be no credible support for the Kuznets hypothesis. And there have been few cases of immiserizing growth.

We then switch from long-run growth to issues of adjustment and transition. Here we argue that the key components linking growth, as a necessary condition for sustained poverty reduction, and adjustment (stabilization plus structural reform), as a necessary condition for aggregate growth recovery, come out strengthened from the recent growth crises and associated reform efforts. Obviously, necessity is not sufficiency, and we do not argue that growth *always* benefits the poor or that *none* of the poor loses from any pro-growth policy reform. But we do contend that macroeconomic adjustment and structural reform are essential for sustainable growth recovery, which in turn is necessary for a sustained reduction in aggregate poverty.

The first two sections of this chapter support and strengthen the case for policies conducive to broad-based economic growth as part of a comprehensive poverty-reduction strategy, as argued in the *World Development Report* on poverty (World Bank 1990) and the associated policy paper (World Bank 1991), *Assistance Strategies to Reduce Poverty.* But a macropolicy environment conducive to growth is not enough. The second part of the poverty-reduction strategy outlined the *World Development Report* — promoting universal access to basic education, health, and social infrastructure (as well as the adoption of social safety nets, particularly in the process of recovery from a low-level growth crisis) — has received added support from new research on the reverse linkage from the initial distribution of assets and income to subsequent growth. We review the evidence that high-inequality countries, such as a number in Latin America and Africa, have lower growth and remain inegalitarian, whereas low-inequality countries, such as many in East Asia, remain egalitarian and achieve rapid poverty reduction from the process of growth.

The theoretical underpinnings of this reverse linkage are only gradually being understood. Some lines of argument originate from political economy considerations: concentration of wealth, such as in land or human capital, leads to policies that protect sectarian interests and impede growth for the rest of society; inequality may also contribute to political instability. Another argument has to do with credit market imperfections, whereby investment in human and physical capital is confined to the owners of initial wealth. The policy implication is that reducing inequality, such as through securing wide access to basic education and health, benefits both the poor immediately and everyone through higher growth. We end by drawing out implications for domestic policy and the IFIs.

The Effect of Growth on Distribution

Recognizing that we are concerned about how the benefits of growth in aggregate incomes are distributed, the question arises as to whether there is any systematic tendency for inequality to change in the process of rising average affluence.[1] This is a long-standing issue in development economics. A still widely held view is that economic growth in low-income countries will necessarily be inequitable, and this view has had considerable influence on thinking about development policy among both advocates and critics of redistributive interventions. By this view, "the rich are usually the first to reap the benefits of national income growth" (Watkins 1995, 34). Here we review the theories and evidence and provide new results based on more recent and improved data.

Kuznets Hypothesis

In his influential argument as to why we might expect inequitable growth in poor countries, Kuznets (1955) claims that inequality will increase in the early stages of growth in a developing country and after some point it will begin to fall; that is, the relationship between inequality (on the vertical axis) and average income (horizontal) will trace out an inverted ∪. Kuznets did not set out a formal theory of why this might happen, but sketched an argument, which has subsequently been formalized. As typically presented, the Kuznets hypothesis assumes that the economy comprises a low-inequality and low-mean rural sector and a richer urban sector with higher inequality. Growth occurs by rural labor's shifting to the urban sector, such that a representative slice of the rural distribution is transformed into a representative slice of the urban distribution. Thus (by assumption), distribution is unchanged within each sector. Starting with the total population in the rural sector, when the first worker moves to the urban sector inequality must increase. And when the last rural worker leaves it must clearly fall again. Between these extremes, the relationship between inequality and average income will follow an inverted ∪.[2]

Kuznets himself was tentative about the hypothesis, yet it has found many supporters since, to the point of being deemed "fully confirmed" by Oshima (1970), a "stylized fact" by Ahluwalia (1976), and an "economic law" by Robinson (1976). Claims of support for the hypothesis can be found in a literature spanning 25 years.[3] We shall argue that the evidence from cross-country data sets has been misleading because of omitted country-level effects. New studies using panel data and within-country time-series data do not support the hypothesis.

Cross-Country Studies
There have been innumerable tests of the Kuznets hypothesis on cross-country data sets by regressing a measure of inequality against a suitable function of average income and seeing if that function follows an inverted ∪. We shall not review the earlier literature here and note only that these tests have typically been ad hoc, with no clear link to the assumptions of the hypothesis. Instead, we focus on a nagging concern about all the tests using cross-country data: that there may be important country-level determinants of inequality (including past inequality) that are correlated with current income levels and so lead to biased estimates. Indeed, such biases could arise solely from differences in the type of data. For example, income is a more common measure for inequality in many middle-income developing countries, notably in Latin America, whereas consumption is more common elsewhere, including among the Asian economies, many of which were closer to the bottom of the income ladder 20 to 30 years ago

when the data used to test the hypothesis were set up. And since consumption inequality is bound to be lower than income inequality due to consumption smoothing, these differences alone would tend to yield an inverted-∪ relationship even if none existed using the same welfare measure. With strong, latent, country-level effects, there can be no guarantee that differences at one point in time will reveal how inequality will evolve with growth.

If such country-level effects were not in fact a problem, then one would expect to see the inverted ∪ reappearing in later country cross sections. So what do data since the mid-1980s suggest about the Kuznets hypothesis? Using data from 63 surveys spanning 1981 through 1992 and covering 44 countries,[4] we tried replicating a number of the specifications for testing the hypothesis typically found in the literature.[5] This was done for both levels and changes over time to eliminate the country-level fixed effect. In no case was there evidence of an inverted ∪, and in no case could one reject the null hypothesis that the regression coefficients were jointly zero. This also confirms earlier results for smaller samples reported by the World Bank (1990), Fields (1989), and Ravallion (1995).[6]

It appears, then, that the cross-country inverted ∪ found in many earlier tests of the hypothesis, mainly using compilations of distributional data for the 1950s to early 1970s, may well have become blurred, or may even have vanished, over time. This probably reflects how various omitted variables have evolved. The new data confirm earlier concerns that these omitted variables were creating an appearance of a cross-country inverted ∪ that had little to do with the hypothesis. We would conjecture that with the growth seen in much of Asia, and the lack of it in much of Africa, the poor and low-inequality countries of 20 to 30 years ago have split in two, blurring the old inverted ∪ but quite possibly better revealing the true relationship.

Further Intertemporal Evidence

To avoid confusing the effects of independent country-specific characteristics (initial conditions) with those of intertemporal changes of policies or economic conditions, arguments for or against the existence of a Kuznets process should ideally be based on time-series evidence. Here we report on two exercises using time-series data. The first draws on data covering 45 developed and developing countries for the years 1947 to 1993. It contains 486 observations on Gini indices.[7] The second makes use of the most extensive time-series data for any single developing country, India.[8]

Table 3.1 gives decade averages of the Gini indices for each of the 45 countries for which reasonably comparable estimates are available for four or more surveys. Although there is clearly variation over time

TABLE 3.1. Gini Indices: Decade Averages, 1960 to Date

Country	Observations	1960s[a]	1970s	1980s	1990s	Trend[b]
Czechoslovakia	10	22.6	20.9	21.1		(−)
Bulgaria	25	22.1	21.9	23.0	27.3	0
Hungary	7	24.4	22.2	22.8		0
Poland	7			25.2		0
Spain	6			25.7		0
United Kingdom	31	25.0	24.3	27.3	32.4	(+)
Former Soviet Union	4			26.0		(+)
Netherlands	9		28.1	28.6		(+)
Taiwan	26	31.2	29.3	29.0	30.5	0
Finland	6		30.7	31.0		0
Canada	23	31.6	31.6	31.5	27.6	0
India	29	31.5	30.9	31.4	31.1	(−)
China	12			31.5	36.2	(+)
New Zealand	11		31.4	34.1		(+)
Sweden	14		33.1	33.7	32.3	0
Indonesia	7		36.6	33.4	33.1	0
Pakistan	6		35.5	33.4		0
Norway	7	36.8	35.3	31.0		(−)
Korea	10	31.5	36.1	35.6		0
Japan	22	35.6	34.1	34.4	35.0	0
Italy	15		37.4	33.4	32.2	(−)
Bangladesh	9	33.5	34.8	37.3		0
United States	45	34.6	34.5	36.9	37.9	(+)
Australia	10	32.0	36.7	36.2	32.5	0
Belgium	8	36.4	42.0	29.6	35.8	0
Portugal	4		40.6	36.8	36.2	0
Germany, Federal Republic	6		36.0	35.8	45.4	(+)
Côte d'Ivoire	5			39.1	41.1	0
Singapore	6		39.0	40.7		0
Venezuela	4		41.5			(−)
Sri Lanka	7	46.0	38.8	43.7		0
Tunisia	5	42.3	44.0	43.0	41.0	0
Philippines	6	42.9	45.3	40.0		0
Hong Kong	10	47.5	41.9	41.4	45.0	0
France	7	48.0	41.6	37.8		(−)
Thailand	8	42.0	41.7	37.8		(+)
Bahamas	11		48.2	44.4	43.0	(−)
Trinidad and Tobago	4		48.5	41.7		0
Costa Rica	5	52.6	46.1	45.1		0
Malaysia	5		51.5	48.0		0
Colombia	5		52.1	51.2		0
Mexico	4	55.3	49.7			(−)
Honduras	5			54.0	52.7	0
Chile	13			54.8	53.1	0
Brazil	7		59.0	55.6		0

Note: The table includes all countries with four or more observations based on national household survey data. All Gini indices are measured for the same indicator (consumption or income) over time for a given country, though it varies between countries. This accounts for some of the cross-country differences, though on adding dummy variables for the type of data in a pooled model one still finds that the bulk of the variation is between countries rather than over time.

[a] Rank correlations of inequality between decades: 1960s–70s, 0.909; 1970s–80s, 0.863; 1980s–90s, 0.849; 1960s–80s, 0.850.

[b] The signs indicate the significance of the Gini time trends (zero indicates no significant trend).

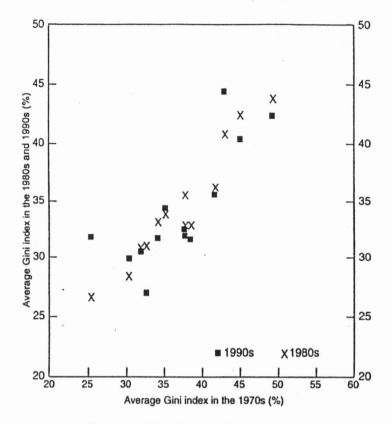

Fig. 3.1.   Gini indices over time by country

(some of which could be differences between surveys or measurement errors), the data suggest substantially greater variation in inequality across countries at a given time than over time for a given country. Indeed, 87 percent of the variance in Gini indices by country and date is accounted for by cross-country variation, whereas only 6 percent is accounted for by variation over time.

The inequality rankings of countries are thus highly stable over the decades; between the 1960s and 1980s, the rank correlation coefficient is 0.85 (table 3.1). Figure 3.1 plots the average Gini index for either the 1980s or 1990s against that for the 1970s. The last column of table 3.1 also gives the direction of the trend;[9] a zero in the final column indicates that the coefficient on time is not significantly different from zero at the 5 percent level, while a plus (or minus) sign indicates that it is significantly positive (negative). Only 17 countries out of 45 have a significant trend in inequality one way or another, and in 12 of the cases its value is small (+ or −0.4 a year).

It would not be correct to conclude from these data that that distribution does not change over time. Even when there is no trend, there is variation, and even seemingly small changes may matter to assessments of overall social progress, including poverty reduction.

What is plain from table 3.1 is that there are strong country effects in inequality, which could well entail appreciable biases in standard tests of the Kuznets hypothesis.[10] For example, if, as table 3.1 suggests, past inequality is an important predictor of current inequality and past inequality influences current incomes, then the standard cross-country regressions used to test the inverted ∪ will be biased.

All this lends support to the view that failure to allow for country effects could be serious. The search for a general law linking growth and inequality must confront the fact that the vast bulk of the variation is among countries, not over time. Further statistical tests on the data set confirm this point. If one allows for country-specific effects, none of the countries in the sample presented in table 3.1 appears to follow the predictions of the Kuznets hypothesis (see Deininger and Squire 1996b for further discussion and analysis).

It is worth reviewing the data for India in more detail because it is one of the most extensive and reliable series and bears on the subsequent discussion. At the time of writing, we could construct distributions of real household consumption expenditures per person in India from 33 nationally representative and reasonably comparable household surveys spanning the period 1951 to 1992.[11] Figure 3.2 plots India's Gini index and net domestic product per person from 1951 to 1991. There was a trend decrease in inequality up to about the mid-1960s but no trend in either direction after that. There is no sign that growth increased inequality, including during the period of higher growth in the 1980s. On running the Anand-Kanbur test equation appropriate to the Gini index, one obtains not an inverted ∪ but an ordinary ∪, though for most of the range of the data, inequality falls as average income increases. However, if one takes first differences of the above equation (so that it is the change in the Gini index between surveys that is regressed on the change in average income and the change in its inverse) then the relationship vanishes. There is no sign in these data that higher growth rates in India put any upward pressure on overall inequality.

Other Lessons from Tests of the Kuznets Hypothesis
The fact that there are such strong country-level effects in distribution does not mean that distribution is unchangeable. Some of the observed variation (across countries and over time) is clearly due to differences in

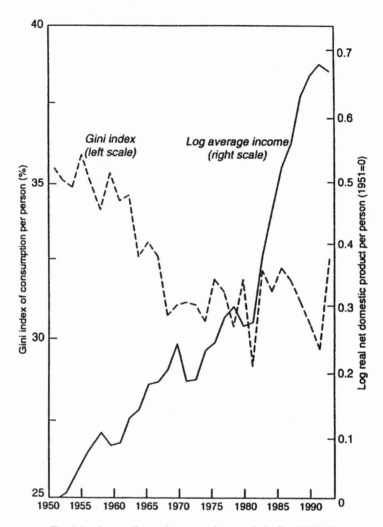

Fig. 3.2.   Inequality and average income in India, 1950–92

the underlying data and measurement errors. But the literature on testing the Kuznets hypothesis has also suggested a number of other factors
that appear to influence inequality and explains at least some of the
omitted country-level effects identified above. Kuznets (1966) specu-
lates on a number of those factors, including shifting intersectoral inequalities, a declining share of (unequally distributed) property income,
and policy changes concerning social security and employment. But on

all these the data base for testing was weak at the time Kuznets was writing. That has changed.

Higher primary and secondary school enrollment rates tend to be associated with lower inequality, and the significance of the income variables tends to diminish when education is taken into account. The quantitative importance of this effect suggests that it may be policy relevant: A 20 percentage point increase in the percentage of the labor force that has at least secondary education increases the share of income received by the bottom 60 percent by between 3 and 4 percentage points (Bourguignon and Morrisson 1990). Papanek and Kyn (1986) find that primary and secondary school enrollment has a quantitatively important effect on the income share received by the poorest 40 percent. By contrast, it is significant but of low quantitative importance in reducing inequality (as measured by the Gini index). Human capital in primary and secondary education had a significant effect on reducing the Gini coefficient in Korea and increasing the share of the bottom 20 percent, whereas university education slightly increased the Gini and did not significantly affect the bottom share of the income distribution (Jung 1992).

Mineral and agricultural exports would be expected to increase inequality to the degree that they produce concentrated rents. This is confirmed for developing countries where a sizable (greater than 5 percent) contribution of mineral exports to gross domestic product (GDP) was associated with 4 to 6 percent decreases of the bottom 40 percent income share (Bourguignon and Morrisson 1990). High importance (greater than 5 percent of GDP) of agricultural exports leads to greater inequality only if such exports are produced on large, rather than on small and medium, farms. By contrast, Papanek and Kyn (1986), using data for developing as well as developed countries, fail to find significant effects, presumably since failure to correct for protection does not allow inferences concerning the international competitiveness of such exports.

Trade theory would predict that protection lowers the reward for the most abundant (most equally distributed) factor of production and increases returns to scarce factors, which are likely to be the more inequitably distributed. Presence of protection indeed seems to worsen income distribution (Bourguignon and Morrisson 1990).

Factor market distortions, whereby there is a wedge between the real wage in the modern sector of the economy and the lower wage in the traditional, mainly agricultural sector, can also influence the extent of inequality. In cross-country comparisons, Bourguignon and Morrisson (1995) find that the extent of economic dualism, as measured by labor productivity in agriculture relative to nonagricultural sectors, tends to increase overall inequality.

There is also evidence for India that the sectoral composition of growth has played a role in the evolution of distribution. Recall that at the aggregate level the data for India reveal little effect of growth on inequality. So which of the Kuznets assumptions do not hold for India? At any one date, both mean that consumption and inequality are higher in urban areas, as Kuznets postulated. The radical departure from his assumptions is in the nature of India's growth process. Growth under the Kuznets hypothesis is driven by rural-to-urban migration, assuming that the means and distributions remain the same within each sector. However, Ravallion and Datt (1996) find that this process has been only a minor source of growth in India, the bulk of which has come from intrasectoral growth; between 1970 and 1990, the Kuznets growth process accounted for only 6 percent of total consumption growth, while growth within the urban and rural sectors accounted for 20 and 74 percent, respectively.

Impact of Growth on Absolute Poverty

The still quite widely held pessimism about the scope for reducing poverty through economic growth has rested in large part on the belief that growth would be inequitable in poor countries. We have surveyed past and new evidence on this view and rejected it as a generalization; there have been cases in which growth was associated with rising inequality, but there have been at least as many cases of falling inequality. There does not appear to be any systematic tendency for distribution to improve or worsen with growth. On average, then, absolute poverty will fall. This is confirmed by the results of a number of recent studies (Fields 1989; World Bank 1990; Squire 1993; Ravallion 1995; Ravallion and Chen 1997). How responsive is poverty to economic growth? Regressing the rates of change in the proportion of the population living on less than one dollar per day against the rate of change in the real value of the survey mean for the 20 countries spanning 1984 through 1993, we obtained a regression coefficient of -2.12 (with a t-ratio of -4.67); thus, a 10 percent increase in the mean can be expected to result in roughly a 20 percent drop in the proportion of people living on less than one dollar per day.[12] This reflects in large part the density of people living on around one dollar per day. But, if we also consider "higher-order" measures of poverty, the effect is even stronger. For the squared poverty gap index proposed by Foster, Greer, and Thorbecke (1984), the corresponding elasticity is even higher at -3.46 ($t = -2.98$).[13] This indicates that the gains are not confined to those near the poverty line. These results confirm those of Ravallion (1995) on a smaller data set.

Somewhat smaller elasticities, but broadly similar results, are obtained if we look at the evolution of poverty over 40 years in India. Over 33 household surveys, the elasticity of the proportion of the population below India's official poverty line and mean consumption is -1.33 ($t = 15.19$). For the squared poverty gap, the elasticity is -2.26 ($t = 10.22$) (Ravallion and Datt 1996).[14]

These elasticities are averages. There is a variation between countries and over time in the extent to which absolute poverty measures respond to growth. Initial distribution is an important factor. Ravallion (1997b) studies the effect on poverty of growth in average incomes during 64 spells (made up of two comparable surveys) across 42 countries in the period 1984 through 1994. He confirms that absolute poverty measures typically respond elastically to growth but also that the elasticity varies markedly with the initial Gini index. A country with a low initial Gini index of about 0.25 can expect an elasticity around -3.3, while a high-inequality country with a Gini of, say, 0.60 could expect an elasticity of only about -1.8.

Growth is only one of the factors that has influenced progress in reducing poverty, albeit it is an important one. Regressions for rates of poverty reduction against rates of growth still leave a sizable share of the variance in country performance unaccounted for by growth. Some of this is measurement error. But measured changes in inequality have a strong independent explanatory power; indeed, rates of poverty reduction respond even more elastically to rates of change in the Gini index than they do to the mean. Regressing the change in the log of the proportion of the population living on less than one dollar per day on the change in the log of the survey mean *and* the change in the log of the Gini index across 20 countries with two reasonably comparable observations in the period 1984 through 1992, one obtains an elasticity to the mean of -2.28 ($t = -6.07$) while the elasticity to the Gini is 3.86 ($t = 3.20$).[15] Even seemingly modest changes in overall inequality can entail sizable changes in the incidence of poverty. When combined with the tests of the "augmented" Kuznets hypotheses discussed earlier, we can postulate a number of other factors that matter through their influence on inequality, including education, the trade regime, and the sectoral composition of growth. We will see whether some or all of these factors might also matter to the poor through their impact on the growth process.

Distributional Effects of Pro-Growth Reforms

So far we have argued that the rate of overall economic growth has no systematic impact on inequality. Yet it has been argued that some of the policy changes advocated as promoting growth increase inequality. For example, real devaluations can promote growth, but they also have an impact on inequality, though the direction of that effect is not obvious on a priori grounds. Here we look more closely at the role played by economy-wide policy changes. In particular, we ask whether the economy-wide factors (including macroeconomic policy changes) that are likely to increase the overall rate of economic growth also have distributional implications.

Adjustment and Transition

For much of the developing world, the 1980s was a period of rapidly rising servicing costs on foreign debt, external terms-of-trade shocks, and fiscal and external imbalances, entailing an unsustainable excess of aggregate demand over supply. Adjustment programs were introduced to help restore macroeconomic balance by combining fiscal contraction — cutting government spending and/or raising taxes — with supply-side measures aimed at reducing inefficiency, such as cutting trade distortions or wasteful parastatals. Unless there is an exceptionally rapid supply-side response, somebody's consumption must fall. The distribution of the burden of adjustment has been one of the most debated issues in development studies over the past decade. The issue has been of even greater significance in the centrally planned economies that are now privatizing and placing much greater reliance on market solutions. What can we say about the impact of adjustment and transition on the poor?

Many countries were not well equipped with relevant household-level data for monitoring welfare impacts of policy reform at the time that adjustment began in the early 1980s. This has improved since. Yet even with good data it can be difficult to isolate the role played by adjustment. Poverty may have risen during an adjustment period, but it may have risen even further without adjustment. Much of the criticism of adjustment policies may have to do with the observation of real hardships that are temporarily incurred at the stabilization stage, yet in all probability would be much greater were the crisis allowed to deepen further. One of the few clear patterns to emerge from the new household-level evidence on the evolution of poverty indicators during adjustment is that the poverty measures tend to move with the mean consumption or income of households, increasing in recession and falling in recovery (Lipton and Ravallion 1995, sec. 5.3).

What happens to the rate of growth in the adjustment to a deep crisis is crucial. In this respect, an important link to likely outcomes for the poor is evident in recent findings of relatively speedy growth recovery (in GDP though not in investment) after a deep inflation (and growth) crisis

(Bruno and Easterly 1995). The median per capita growth rate in a group of 13 countries successfully stabilizing from more than 40 percent inflation shifted from −4 percent in the years up to and including the first year after stabilization to 1.5 percent in the second year, and to close to 4 percent in the third year and beyond. Even when aggregate growth remains temporarily negative as inflation already falls, it is not at all clear which way the distributional outcome goes; income groups whose nominal income is not tied to inflation or whose income taxes are withheld at the source will gain in relative terms as inflation falls drastically.[16]

The distributional impacts of adjustment depend on the economy's initial conditions, including its openness, and the extent of flexibility in its output and factor markets, thus pointing to the importance of market reforms as an important conditioning environment. Actual experiences in distributional shifts during adjustment have been diverse. In the Philippines, adverse distributional effects resulted in higher poverty despite modest growth in the late 1980s (Balisacan 1993). A small improvement in distribution helped the poor during adjustment in Indonesia during the mid-1980s (Ravallion and Huppi 1991). Dorosh and Sahn (1993) argue that the distributional effects of real devaluations will tend to be pro-poor in a number of African countries, since the rural poor tend to be net producers of tradables.[17] The diversity of initial conditions warns against generalizations on the distributional impacts of adjustment.

A common presumption is that countries under shock face a dynamic tradeoff; living standards may fall in the short term during adjustment (relative to nonadjustment), but they will rise in the longer term. This tradeoff, however, could well be overstated. For example, Peru initially avoided adjustment, and poverty rose sharply between 1985 and 1990 (Glewwe and Hall 1994). Yet the subsequent period of more orthodox reforms between 1991 and 1994 quickly saw positive growth and falling poverty measures (Favaro and MacIsaac 1995).

Evidence from Three Regions

In this section, we review the evidence now available for sub-Saharan Africa and Latin America, the two regions most closely associated with adjustment, and then turn to the evidence for the transition economies of Eastern Europe and the former Soviet Union.

New, encouraging results have emerged for some countries in Africa. Demery and Squire (1996) use household survey data at two points of time in the mid-1980s to early 1990s to assess the change in poverty in the six African countries for which such data are available. They find that the five countries experiencing improvement in an index measuring performance in fiscal, exchange rate, and monetary policies also saw poverty decline, whereas the one country in the sample that witnessed a deteriorating policy performance suffered increased poverty (table 3.2).

These results cannot be extrapolated to the rest of the continent; policy implementation varied widely, and on balance poverty has almost certainly increased.[18] Nor can it be concluded that all the poor benefited in the countries that saw declining poverty on average; the surveys reveal that some among the poor suffered greater deprivation. And it cannot be claimed that causality from macroeconomic policy to poverty has been established. Nevertheless, the data do confirm that improvements in macroeconomic policy are consistent with declines in poverty, even in the short run. This is, in turn, consistent with evidence on growth; poverty fell where growth was positive and increased where growth was negative. Indeed, Demery and Squire (1996) show that the change in poverty was determined primarily by the change in mean income, with changes in inequality playing a secondary role and, at least in this sample, working in the opposite direction to growth as far as the poor are concerned.

In the Latin American context, Morley (1994) has similarly recorded a close relationship between growth and outcomes for the poor in the adjustment process. Reviewing periods of recession (falling per capita income for at least two years) and periods of recovery, he finds that poverty increased in 55 of the 58 cases of recession and fell in 22 of the 32 recoveries. Contrary to the results from the sample of six African countries, Morley finds that recessions were accompanied by rising inequality (the poor suffered doubly), while recoveries were associated with falling inequality (the poor benefited doubly). But, as in the African sample, the changes in poverty could be attributed mainly to changes in mean income.

Evidence now appearing for the transition economies of Eastern Europe and the former Soviet Union again points to the importance of

TABLE 3.2. **Macroeconomic Policy and Poverty in Africa**

Country	Change in Poor (percentage points per annum)	Change in Macropolicy (weighted score of macropolicy variables)
Côte d'Ivoire	+5.30	−1.65
Kenya	−0.28	+0.45
Nigeria	−1.27	+1.79
Tanzania	−1.83	+2.76
Ghana	−1.95	+1.35
Ethiopia	−3.60	+0.55

Source: Demery and Squire 1996.

changes in aggregate GDP but also to a systematic trend toward greater inequality. As might be expected, the large drops in GDP in these countries have been reflected in substantially higher levels of poverty. What is more interesting is the tendency toward greater inequality. These countries began the period with some of the lowest Gini coefficients in the world. The transition has entailed consistent association between growth and inequality: both deteriorated (Milanovic 1995; Ravallion and Chen 1997).

Thus, we find evidence of a systematic worsening of inequality in the transition economies as GDP has declined but observe no simple relationship between growth and inequality in the adjusting countries, although the shifts in the Gini coefficient at least in Africa appear to have been larger during the adjustment phase than during periods of stable growth. We conclude that successful adjustment usually leads to growth recovery, which in general will also reduce poverty. We end, though, with two qualifications.

First, the detailed policy response, particularly in the composition of public expenditure cuts, can greatly affect the poverty outcomes of adjustment. In some cases, aggregate budget contraction has been combined with rising shares (and occasionally rising absolute levels) of public spending in the social sectors, including targeted transfers (Ribe et al. 1990; World Bank 1990, chap. 7; Selowsky 1991). In Indonesia, the careful mix of public spending cuts during adjustment and the rapid currency devaluations helped mitigate the short-term consequences for the poor of declining growth (Thorbecke 1991). Maintaining public infrastructure can also be crucial to the success of reform programs. The fiscal crunch often tempts governments to cut these infrastructural sectors. There is another lesson here for the nature of fiscal retrenchment during stabilization.

Second, we have said nothing about other dimensions of poverty, including human development, which may not be adequately reflected in income- or consumption-based measures (Sen 1992). It is beyond our scope to go deeply into the nonincome dimensions of welfare. There is evidence that progress in reducing income poverty is instrumentally crucial to progress against most nonincome dimensions of poverty but that incomes are not all that matter. Indeed, for some nonincome dimensions of welfare, command over market goods may well be secondary to command over key, publicly provided social services, notably access to basic health care and schooling.[19] Cross-country comparisons also suggest that public health spending in developing countries generally matters more to the health of the poor than the nonpoor (Bidani and Ravallion 1997). Cuts in key categories of social spending during adjustment can entail heavy burdens on poor people in both the short and the long runs.

The Effect of Distribution on Growth

So far we have looked at how growth might alter distribution. We now consider the possibility of a reverse causation. There are a number of ways in which this could happen.[20] We focus on two, credit constraints and political economy, which have potential implications for the accumulation of capital, especially human capital, and growth. The first affects the access of the poor to education, and the second affects incentives and the returns to education.

Credit, Distribution, and Growth

By preventing the poor from making productive investments (such as schooling), credit constraints arising, for example, from asymmetric information perpetuate a low and inequitable growth process. Furthermore, the more inequitable the initial distribution (and, hence, the greater the number of poor and typically credit-constrained people), the more severe this effect will be. A number of authors have examined credit market imperfections in general equilibrium models with lumpy investment (Banerjee and Newman 1993; Tsiddon 1992; Saint-Paul and Verdier 1992; Galor and Zeira 1993). The main result is that where credit market constraints prevent the poor from making productive indivisible investments, inequalities in the wealth distribution can have significant negative impacts on growth. What can policy do? Here we review three possible actions: provision of credit, redistribution of assets, and tax-subsidy interventions.

Intervention in credit markets aimed at channeling credit directly to rationed groups by means of subsidized interest rates may well reduce growth even further. In a dynamic perspective, such interventions are likely to cause efficiency-decreasing distortions and rent-seeking behavior, thus further reducing efficiency and equity (Bencivenga and Smith 1991).

An alternative approach entails equalizing the distribution of assets, to increase the poor's ownership of capital directly and their access to credit markets. A large number of analytical models have stressed the importance of the initial distribution of endowments and the potentially large increases in social welfare that could be gained by an initial redistribution of assets (including Banerjee and Newman 1993 and Chatterjee 1991). Evidence from Asian countries (Japan, Taiwan, and Korea), where externally imposed land reform was followed by high growth, appears to support the hypothesis. But in many situations such redistribution may be possible only with full compensation. Whether, and under what circumstances, such schemes will then pass the scrutiny of careful evaluation has yet to be determined.[21] There are often less ambitious but still potentially important opportunities for giving poor farmers greater security of tenure in places where land rights are ill defined.

If the informational imperfections that cause credit rationing cannot be eliminated, governments can seek ways around them by subsidizing education and taxing future wages. Assuming that higher education is reflected in higher lifetime earnings, governments can provide subsidies to schooling and finance them through a tax on future earnings without having to deal with the problems involved in identifying individual ability (Hoff and Lyon 1994). It can be shown that policies mandating compulsory schooling, financed by a proportional tax on wage income, increase economic growth and, by redistributing from agents with high human capital endowment to those with less, make the intragenerational distribution of income more equal (Eckstein and Zilcha 1994). Where it is very difficult to identify the type of individual agents ex ante, or if access to credit markets is highly unequal, such policies can be desirable.

Political Economy

The discussion suggests that among economies characterized by credit rationing those with a more equal distribution of wealth will accumulate more human capital and grow faster than those marked by a more inegalitarian distribution. High inequality will also make it easier to adopt distortionary policies that will negatively affect individuals' investment decisions, stifle growth, and conceivably generate political instability.

The most common mechanism used to establish a link between political forces and economic outcomes is the notion of the median voter. According to this argument, the median voter's distance from the average capital endowment in the economy will increase with wealth inequality, thus leading him or her to support a capital tax rate that is higher the more unequal the distribution of wealth is. This, in turn, would reduce incentives for investment in physical and human capital, resulting in lower growth.

The median voter model, however, is not a plausible description of the political process governing decision making in many developing countries. An alternative mechanism relies on lobbying. Greater wealth allows the rich to spend more resources on lobbying activities to obtain differential treatment. In the extreme form, the ability to lobby would be directly proportional to the amount of economic assets owned by an individual. A model that uses this assumption is provided by Persson and Tabellini (1994), who draw a connection between high concentration of land, landowners' ability to lobby government successfully for preferential tax treatment of this asset, and the ensuing overinvestment in land.

Such disproportionate taxation of nonlandowning groups leads to increasing inequality over time and to slower growth.

Inequality of asset ownership is also at the root of the many models that relate inflation to inequality of the distribution of income. The key idea is that inflation imposes losses on certain groups and that such losses are distributed very inequitably. Inflation taxes holders of money assets (the rich), but their access to foreign currency and capital flight allows them to shift the burden of inflation to the poor. This opens not only the possibility for the rich to "park" their assets abroad and then approve inflationary policies (financed by the poor), but it could also form the basis for strategic behavior of the rich (in support of "populist" policies), which could give rise to the typical stop-and-go policy cycles observed in many Latin American countries (Laban and Sturzenegger 1994). Similarly, Özler and Tabellini (1991) model the class struggle of workers, capital, and the government and — based on the capitalists' ability to invest in a risk-free foreign asset at the world interest rate — show a broad range of situations where domestic investment and growth would be negatively associated with inequality in the distribution of assets.

In contrast to median voter models, lobbying models can incorporate dynamic effects and strategic behavior. If politicians are self-interested, the ability of the rich to offer high bribes, and the inability of the poor to resist taxation, can lead to path-dependent equilibria (Brainard and Verdier 1994); for example, industries affected by a negative shock may choose whether to adjust or to lobby for protection, depending on the type of politician in power. Adjustment will be slower the more responsive politicians are to lobbying; in this case, growth-reducing policy interventions would be expected to increase with overall wealth inequality.

Recent models have emphasized that major policy decisions, particularly the adoption of macroeconomic stabilization measures, can be understood in the framework of a bargaining game between different social groups. Many factors beyond the distribution of income can influence bargaining power, but income distribution plays an important role. Models that describe economic stabilization as a strategic game between the rich and the poor show that stabilization, being associated with an increase in aggregate productivity, is more likely to be delayed the greater the inequality of the income distribution (Alesina and Drazen 1991). The reason is that an unequal distribution of income (or differential access to "financial technology," which could be used to diversify risk) implies that waiting reduces the utility of the rich only marginally while imposing large costs on the poor. This would in turn increase the probability that in the end the poor will give in and shoulder all the cost of adjustment. The model can also be used to show that even if (often under external pressure or acute fiscal crisis) adjustment measures are adopted the lack of social consensus or the perception by some groups that they have to pay a disproportionate share of adjustment costs may lead to backsliding as soon as the external pressures subside (Laban and Sturzenegger 1994).

Evidence

The arguments reviewed suggest that greater income inequality will lead to lower investment in physical and human capital and, hence, to slower growth. There have been a number of recent attempts to test this hypothesis. Data quality is unusually worrying here. Although household survey methods have improved greatly in the past 10 to 15 years, a large question mark must be attached to the quality and comparability of the historical data on distribution in the 1950s, 1960s, and 1970s, which have been used to test the impact of initial distribution on growth.[22] Furthermore, unlike the tests of the Kuznets hypothesis, the noisy inequality variable is now on the right-hand side, so there must be a general presumption that standard estimators will give biased results. Although these and other issues of data and econometric specification should not be underrated, they take us beyond our present scope.[23]

The tests that have been reported in recent literature confirm a negative impact of initial inequality on growth in both developed and developing Persson and Tabellini countries (Alesina and Rodrik 1994; Persson and Tabellini 1994; Clarke 1995). For a sample of nine OECD countries, analysis of 20-year growth rates starting from 1830 shows that the income share of the top quintile is negatively related to growth; it explains about 20 percent of the variance of growth rates across countries, and an increase of one standard deviation in this share decreases the Persson and Tabellini growth rate by half a percentage point (Persson and Tabellini 1994). For a sample of developing and developed countries, Clarke (1995) shows a robust relationship between initial inequality and growth that holds for different econometric specifications. On an expanded and (almost certainly) higher quality data set, Deininger and Squire (1996b) confirm significant adverse effects of higher initial income and (especially) land inequality on subsequent growth rates controlling for other factors normally expected to influence growth rates. The empirical prediction that high inequality in landownership is associated with lower capital accumulation and growth is also confirmed by Persson and Tabellini (1994). There is also evidence from a cross section of 70 countries for the period 1960 through 1985 that economic inequality increases political instability and reduces physical capital investment (Alesina and Perotti 1993).

But the verdict is not yet in on how strong or robust the impact is of initial inequality on future growth. For example, in one test Fishlow (1996) reports no significant effect once one controls for Latin America (with simultaneously high inequality and low growth for much of the period).[24] As in tests of the Kuznets hypothesis, there are some strong regional effects in the cross-sectional relationship, though that fact alone does not mean the relationship is spurious. Like the Kuznets hypothesis, the real test will be in how the regional effects evolve. Further empirical work is needed, and the better distributional data now available should stimulate future research on this issue.

Conclusions

The "stylized fact" that distribution must get worse in poor countries before it can get better turns out not to be a fact at all. Effects of growth on inequality can go either way and are contingent on a number of other factors. There is little sign in the new cross-country data we assembled of any systematic impact of growth on inequality. Possibly measurement errors are confounding the true relationship, but we think it more likely that the relationship between growth and distribution is by no means as simple as some theories in development economics have postulated.

If distribution is unchanged, then growth will reduce absolute poverty. Indeed, absolute poverty measures typically respond quite elastically to growth in average incomes, and the benefits are certainly not, as a rule, confined to those near the poverty line.

One should be clear about what can and cannot be concluded from our results. It would not be correct to say that growth *always* benefits the poor or that *none* of the poor lose from pro-growth policy reforms. Here we are looking only at broad aggregates. Cases of sufficiently adverse distributional impacts to wipe out the aggregate gains to the poor are unusual, if not rare. But there can be large differences between countries in the extent to which growth reduces absolute poverty. The gains to poor people will tend to be lower the higher the extent of initial inequality. And even in countries with initially low inequality and a growth process that brings rapid and sizable gains to most of the poor some will not be in a position to take advantage of the new opportunities and some may well lose. There can be an important role here for compensatory direct interventions, providing they are well integrated into the general policy framework, in keeping with overall fiscal and monetary discipline.

Nor does the evidence suggest that growth is always distribution neutral. Roughly half the time, inequality rises, and half the time it falls.

And it would also be wrong to conclude that changes in distribution are of little consequence. Indeed, we find that poverty measures respond quite elastically to changes in distribution. The point is not that distribution is irrelevant or that it never changes, but rather that its changes are generally uncorrelated with economic growth.

There are arguments as to why initial distribution matters for the nature and extent of subsequent growth. As a general rule, a more equal initial distribution will entail that a given rate of growth will be more pro-poor. It has also been argued that it will result in a higher rate of growth. This link can operate through credit market constraints by limiting the ability of the poor to invest. The negative effect on growth is strengthened if distortionary policy interventions in favor of the rich further undermine the poor's incentives to invest. The empirical evidence on these effects is as yet mixed, though the recent literature does not support a view that higher initial inequality allows a higher rate of growth. Some studies suggest no effect, and others suggest that high inequality inhibits growth.

Thus, there does not appear to be any intrinsic overall tradeoff between long-run efficiency and equity. In particular, policies aimed at facilitating accumulation of productive assets by the poor, when adopted in a relatively nondistorted framework, are also important instruments for achieving higher growth. The problem should not be posed as one of choosing between growth and redistribution.

When we put these two halves together—one on the impact of growth on distribution and one on the reverse causation—we can begin to see the structure and some of the details of a joint model of distribution and growth and, hence, of poverty. The extent to which this is a truly simultaneous model is a moot point; distribution may well affect growth more than growth affects distribution, though this interrelationship is still being researched. There is also a dynamic state-dependent structure to this joint model in which initial conditions (of average incomes, inequality, and other factors) matter. Within this structure, a common set of policy-relevant explanatory variables can be identified, with basic education one of the more robust predictors of both variables; higher proportions of men and women with good basic schooling entail a better distribution of a larger total income.

Countries that give priority to basic human capabilities in schooling, health, and nutrition not only directly contribute to well-being but are also more likely to see improving income distributions and higher average incomes over the longer term. There are often also ways in which governments can help relieve the credit constraints facing the poor, though even means-tested credit subsidies may not be the best way. Reducing transaction costs and helping people organize themselves have often proved to be better approaches. A more equitable distribution of physical assets, notably land, can also help greatly (both directly and by relieving credit constraints on investment by poor people), though the policy implications are not as straightforward as with health and education. The sectoral composition of economic growth has also been emphasized as an important factor. Sectoral biases against the rural sector in pricing, exchange rates, and public investment are not in the interests of either higher growth or better distribution. Sound macroeconomic policies appear to be essential for sustained growth; they either have no systematic effect on distribution or have potentially adverse short-term impacts that typically are not strong enough to outweigh the gains to the poor from growth. Paying attention to the composition of public expenditures in the adjustment program and to the inclusion of effective safety nets for the poor will help improve the distributional outcome in the transition to a pro-poor growth recovery.

Some of the key factors in achieving an equitable growth path, such as better schooling, also raise the living standards of poor people in both the income and nonincome dimensions. The nature of the dynamic interaction of initial conditions with future growth and distributional change can also have important policy implications. Countries with poor initial conditions (due, in part, to past policies) will tend to diverge from the rest. It may be possible to overcome this only if the lagging countries can get a large enough jump start, and here there may be an especially important role for international development assistance, since private capital flows usually come in only at a later stage of the reform process. There will undoubtedly remain areas of social policy or infrastructure in which private capital will not participate, even after successful reform.

The upshot of all that we know is that promoting growth is good because it is a potentially, and, in most cases, an actually, important vehicle for improving the living standards at all levels, and we now have a better idea about the policies that lead to growth, ranging from the fundamental institutional and market incentives to the promotion of macrostability. These policies should be pursued in all countries, but we suspect that these will be less effective or less well implemented in high-inequality countries. Reducing inequality is good because it will benefit the poor both immediately and in the longer term through a more pro-poor and probably higher growth rate.

Apart from the details of structural and macropolicy interventions that have already been mentioned, there are two major aspects that our analysis highlights for the changing role of the IFIs. First, there is an important implication in the area of greater selectivity among countries. Obviously, the IFIs should support growth-promoting policies in all countries, but the focus should be on countries that are clearly committed to reform. It appears that low-inequality countries may well be more likely to be responsive to the need for reforms and more able to implement them in a shared-growth fashion. Testing commitment in high-inequality countries would seem especially important. Actions that are both growth promoting and equity enhancing may be the only realistic solution, but even this solution, experience shows, does not necessarily guarantee sustainability. The second important implication comes from the externality that appears to be associated with improvement in the distribution of assets and income: future generations benefit because future growth will tend to be higher through better policies and better access to credit markets. If further research establishes the strength and robustness of this result, then it has an important policy implication: The IFIs should be willing to subsidize actions that encourage redistribution, especially investment in basic education and land reform.

NOTES

For their helpful comments, we are grateful to the discussants, Jiwei Lou, Jacob Mwanza, and Dani Rodrik, as well as other conference participants, and to Klaus Deininger, Peter Lanjouw, Andrés Solimano, Jack van Holst Pellekaan, Dominique van de Walle, Holger Wolf, and Shlomo Yitzhaki. The views set out in this chapter are those of the authors and should not be attributed to the World Bank.

1. There are numerous measures of inequality that might be considered compelling, and in principle they can diverge greatly in their assessments of whether distribution has improved. In practice, however, for many of the purposes of measurement there appears to be considerable congruence among a number of these measures. We will rely heavily here on the most widely used summary statistic on distribution, the Gini index. There is also the question: inequality of what? Here we focus mainly on current income or consumption inequality; both may diverge from other measures that might be compelling, such as inequality in lifetime utility or inequality in "capabilities" (on the latter, see Sen 1992).

2. See Anand and Kanbur 1993 for a more precise formulation and necessary and sufficient conditions for the inverted $\cup$ for six possible inequality measures.

3. An influential early example was Adelman and Morris 1973. At the time of writing, the most recent example we know of is Ram 1995.

4. This is the same data set used in Chen, Datt, and Ravallion 1994, which gives details.

5. We tried regressing the Gini index against a quadratic function of mean consumption (both linear and logs) as well as the Anand and Kanbur (1993) specification in which the Gini is regressed on the mean and the reciprocal of the mean. We also tried the specification proposed by Ram (1955) in

which a quadratic function of the mean is used but with the intercept suppressed. This test did suggest an inverted ∪, but it appears to have very low power to reject the Kuznets hypothesis; indeed, on suppressing the intercept, one will find an inverted ∪ between any two independent random variables with positive means (Ravallion 1997a).

6. The latter allows for fixed country-level effects. Fields and Jakubson (1992) find that the inverted ∪ "flips" to an ordinary ∪ when one allows for fixed effects, but our data do not confirm this finding.

7. See Deininger and Squire 1996a for further details.

8. See Ravallion and Datt 1996.

9. These are based on ordinary least-squares estimates of the coefficient on time.

10. These effects may entail either an omitted dynamic effect of past inequality or some other omitted country-level fixed effect in the error term. Either will bias standard tests on cross sections of country data.

11. The surveys were done by India's National Sample Survey Organization (NSSO). To form the national distributions of real consumption from the NSSO tabulations of nominal expenditure distributions, an allowance was made for urban-rural cost-of-living differences and for differences in the rate of inflation between urban and rural areas (for details, see Datt 1996).

12. It might be argued that this correlation is partly spurious, since both the survey mean and the poverty index were estimated from the same data. If instead we use an instrumental variables estimator, using the growth rate in GDP per capita between the survey dates as the instrument, then we get a very similar result: an elasticity of -2.15 (t-ratio $= -3.24$). Since the national accounts and census are largely independent of the household surveys, our estimate of the elasticity appears to be robust.

13. The corresponding instrumental variables estimate is -4.11 ($t = -2.36$).

14. Using the rate of growth in consumption per person from the national accounts as an instrument, the instrumental variables estimates are -1.47 ($t = 6.51$) for the head count index and -2.51 ($t = 4.50$) for the squared poverty gap.

15. The elasticity to changes in the Gini index is even higher if one uses a measure of poverty that better reflects distribution among the poor; using the "squared poverty gap" index, the elasticity to the Gini rises to 8.07 ($t = 2.49$), while the elasticity to the mean is -3.79 ($t = -3.61$).

16. This, for example, was the case for wage earners as against profit earners in the Israeli stabilization of 1985. Measurement is complicated by the fact that inflation during the household survey period will generally put an upward bias on inequality measures defined on nominal incomes (Kakwani 1987); conversely, stabilization will impart a downward bias.

17. Lipton and Ravallion (1995) review other recent arguments and evidence on the impacts of adjustment on the poor.

18. See Chen, Datt, and Ravallion (1994), who also show that countries without adequate poverty data tend also to have worse macroperformance, so compilations of available poverty data may well understate the problem.

19. On these issues, see Anand and Ravallion 1993 and Bidani and Ravallion 1997.

20. Generally, when markets are incomplete there will be efficiency implications of changes in distribution (Hoff 1994). Some specific examples in the literature are reviewed in Lipton and Ravallion 1995, sec. 5.1. The following discussion draws in part on Deininger and Squire 1996b.

21. Ongoing World Bank involvement in market-assisted land reform operations in South Africa and Colombia would provide an opportunity to test this empirically.

22. Some of the "data points" in these older compilations were not even based on household surveys but were synthetic estimates, and the quality of the survey data sets used was highly variable. For an overview of these issues, see Fields 1994. Recent compilations have gone some way toward eliminating these problems (Chen, Datt, and Ravallion 1994; Deininger and Squire 1996a).

23. The inclusion of the initial average income variable on the right-hand side of these equations explaining the rate of growth also raises concerns about bias in the ordinary least-squares estimators widely used in this literature.

24. Nonetheless Clarke (1995) and Deininger and Squire (1996b) report that the inequality effect on growth is robust to this and other changes in specification.

REFERENCES

Adelman, Irma, and Cynthia Taft Morris. 1973. *Economic Growth and Social Equity in Developing Countries.* Stanford: Stanford University Press.

Adelman, Irma, and Sherman Robinson. 1988. "Income Distribution and Development." In H. Chenery and T. N. Srinivasan, eds., *Handbook of Development Economics,* 2: chap. 19. Rotterdam: North-Holland.

Ahluwalia, Montek S. 1976. "Income Distribution and Development: Some Stylized Facts." *American Economic Review Papers and Proceedings* 66: 128–35.

Alesina, Alberto, and Allan Drazen. 1991. "Why Are Stabilizations Delayed?" *American Economic Review* 81:1170–88.

Alesina, Alberto, and Roberto Perotti. 1993. *Income Distribution, Political Instability, and Investment.* Working Paper no. 4,486. Cambridge, MA: National Bureau of Economic Research.

Alesina, Alberto, and Dani Rodrik. 1994. "Distributive Politics and Economic Growth." *Quarterly Journal of Economics* 109:465–90.

Anand, Sudhir, and S. M. Ravi Kanbur. 1993. "The Kuznets Process and the Inequality-Development Relationship." *Journal of Development Economics* 40:25–52.

Anand, Sudhir, and Martin Ravallion. 1993. "Human Development in Poor Countries: On the Role of Private Incomes and Public Services." *Journal of Economic Perspectives* 7:133–50.

Balisacan, Arsenio M. 1993. "Anatomy of Poverty during Adjustment: The

Case of the Philippines." *Economic Development and Cultural Change* 44:33–62.

Banerjee, Abhijit V., and Andrew F. Newman. 1993. "Occupational Choice and the Process of Development." *Journal of Political Economy* 101: 272–98.

Bencivenga, Valerie, and Bruce Smith. 1991. "Financial Intermediation and Endogenous Growth." *Review of Economic Studies* 58:195–209.

Bidani, Benu, and Martin Ravallion. 1997. "Decomposing Social Indicators Using Distributional Data." *Journal of Econometrics* 77:125–39.

Bourguignon, François, and C. Morrisson. 1990. "Income Distribution, Development, and Foreign Trade: A Cross-Sectional Analysis." *European Economic Review* 34:1113–32.

———. 1995. *Inequality and Development: The Role of Dualism.* Document 95–32. Paris: DELTA.

Brainard, S. Lael, and Thierry Verdier. 1994. "Lobbying and Adjustment in Declining Industries." *European Economic Review* 38:586–95.

Bruno, Michael, and William Easterly. 1995. *Inflation Crises and Long-Run Growth.* Policy Research Working Paper no. 1,517. Washington, DC: World Bank.

Chatterjee, S. 1991. *The Effect of Transitional Dynamics on the Distribution of Wealth in a Neoclassical Capital Accumulation Model.* Working Paper no. 91–22. Philadelphia: Federal Reserve Bank of Philadelphia.

Chen, Shaohua, Gaurav Datt, and Martin Ravallion. 1994. "Is Poverty Increasing or Decreasing in the Developing World?" *Review of Income and Wealth* 40:359–76.

Chenery, H., M. Ahluwalia, C. Bell, J. Duloy, and R. Jolly. 1974. *Redistribution with Growth.* Oxford: Oxford University Press.

Clarke, George R. G. 1995. "More Evidence on Income Distribution and Growth." *Journal of Development Economics* 47:403–27.

Datt, Gaurav. 1996. "Poverty in India, 1951–1992: Trends and Decompositions." Policy Research Department, World Bank. Mimeo.

Datt, Gaurav, and Martin Ravallion. 1992. "Growth and Redistribution Components of Changes in Poverty Measures: A Decomposition with Applications to Brazil and India in the 1980s." *Journal of Development Economics* 38:275–95.

Deininger, Klaus, and Lyn Squire. 1996a. "A New Data Set for Measuring Income Inequality." *World Bank Economic Review* 10:565–92.

———. 1996b. "New Ways of Looking at Old Issues: Growth and Inequality." Policy Research Department, World Bank. Mimeo.

Demery, Lionel, and Lyn Squire. 1996. "Macroeconomic Adjustment and Poverty in Africa: An Emerging Picture." *World Bank Research Observer* 11(1) (February): 39–60.

Dorosh, Paul A., and David E. Sahn. 1993. "A General Equilibrium Analysis of the Effect of Macroeconomic Adjustment on Poverty in Africa." Cornell University Food and Nutrition Policy Program. Mimeo.

Eckstein, Zvi, and Itzhak Zilcha. 1994. "The Effects of Compulsory Schooling on Growth Income Distribution and Welfare." *Journal of Public Economics* 54:339–59.

Favaro, Edgardo, and Donna MacIsaac. 1995. "Who Benefited from Peru's Reform Program? Poverty Note." Latin America 3 Country Department, World Bank. Mimeo.

Fields, Gary. 1989. "Changes in Poverty and Inequality in Developing Countries." *World Bank Research Observer* 4:167–85.

———. 1994. "Data for Measuring Poverty and Inequality Changes in the Developing Countries." *Journal of Development Economics* 44:87–102.

Fields, Gary, and George Jakubson. 1992. "New Evidence on the Kuznets Curve." Cornell University. Mimeo.

Fishlow, Albert. 1996. "Inequality, Poverty, and Growth: Where Do We Stand?" In Michael Bruno and Boris Pleskovic, eds., *Annual World Bank Conference on Development Economics, 1995.* Washington, DC: World Bank.

Foster, James, J. Greer, and E. Thorbecke. 1984. "A Class of Decomposable Poverty Measures." *Econometrica* 52:761–66.

Galor, Oded, and Joseph Zeira. 1993. "Income Distribution and Macroeconomics." *Review of Economic Studies* 60:35–52.

Glewwe, Paul, and Gillette Hall. 1994. "Poverty, Inequality, and Living Standards during Unorthodox Adjustment: The Case of Peru." *Economic Development and Cultural Change* 42:689–717.

Hoff, Karla. 1994. "The Second Theorem of the Second Best." *Journal of Public Economics* 54:223–42.

Hoff, Karla, and Andrew B. Lyon. 1994. *Non-leaky Buckets: Optimal Redistributive Taxation and Agency Costs.* Working Paper no. 4,652. Cambridge, MA: National Bureau of Economic Research.

Jung, Jin Hwa. 1992. "Personal Income Distribution in Korea, 1963–1986: A Human Capital Approach." *Journal of Asian Economics* 3:57–72.

Kakwani, Nanak. 1987. "Inequality of Income Derived from Survey Data during the Inflationary Period." *Economics Letters* 23:387–88.

Kuznets, Simon. 1955. "Economic Growth and Income Inequality." *American Economic Review* 45:1–28.

———. 1966. *Modern Economic Growth.* New Haven: Yale University Press.

Laban, Raul, and Federico Sturzenegger. 1994. "Distributional Conflict, Financial Adaptation, and Delayed Stabilizations." *Economics and Politics* 6: 257–76.

Lipton, Michael, and Martin Ravallion. 1995. "Poverty and Policy." In Jere Behrman and T. N. Srinivasan, eds., *Handbook of Development Economics,* 3: chap. 4. Amsterdam: North-Holland.

Milanovic, Branko. 1995. *Poverty, Inequality, and Social Policy in Transition Economies.* Research Paper no. 9. Washington, DC: World Bank, Transition Economics Division.

Morley, Samuel A. 1994. *Poverty and Inequality in Latin America: Past Evidence, Future Prospects.* Policy Essay no. 13. Washington, DC: Overseas Development Council.

Oshima, H. 1970. "Income Inequality and Economic Growth: The Post-war Experience of Asian Countries." *Malayan Economic Review* 15:7–41.

Özler, S., and G. Tabellini. 1991. *External Debt and Political Instability.* Working Paper no. 3,772. Cambridge, MA: National Bureau of Economic Research.

Papanek, Gustav, and Oldrich Kyn. 1986. "The Effect on Income Distribution of Development, the Growth Rate, and Economic Strategy." *Journal of Development Economics* 23:55–65.

Persson, Torsten, and Guido Tabellini. 1994. "Is Inequality Harmful for Growth?" *American Economic Review* 84:600–21.

Ram, Rati. 1995. "Economic Development and Inequality: An Overlooked Regression Constraint." *Economic Development and Cultural Change* 3: 425–34.

Ravallion, Martin. 1995. "Growth and Poverty: Evidence for the Developing World." *Economics Letters* 48:411–17.

———. 1997a. "A Comment on Rati Ram's Test of the Kuznets Hypothesis." *Economic Development and Cultural Change.* 46, no. 1: 187–90.

———. 1997b. "Can High-Inequality Developing Countries Escape Absolute Poverty?" *Economics Letters.*

Ravallion, Martin, and Shaohua Chen. 1997. "What Can New Survey Data Tell Us About Recent Changes in Living Standards in Developing and Transitional Economies?" *World Bank Economic Review* 11 (May): 357–82.

Ravallion, Martin, and Gaurav Datt. 1996. "How Important to India's Poor Is the Sectoral Composition of Growth?" *World Bank Economic Review* 10: 1–25.

Ravallion, Martin, and Monika Huppi. 1991. "Measuring Changes in Poverty: A Methodological Case Study of Indonesia during an Adjustment Period." *World Bank Economic Review* 5:57–82.

Ribe, Helena, S. Carvalho, R. Liebenthal, P. Nicholas, and E. Zuckerman. 1990. *How Adjustment Programs Can Help the Poor.* World Bank Discussion Paper no. 71. Washington, DC: World Bank.

Robinson, Sherman. 1976. "A Note on the U-Hypothesis Relating Income Inequality and Economic Development." *American Economic Review* 66: 437–40.

Saint-Paul, Gilles, and Thierry Verdier. 1992. "Historical Accidents and the Persistence of Distributional Conflicts." *Journal of the Japanese and International Economies* 6:406–22.

Selowsky, Marcelo. 1991. "Protecting Nutrition Status in Adjustment Programs: Recent World Bank Activities and Projects in Latin America." *Food and Nutrition Bulletin* 13:293–302.

Sen, Amartya. 1992. *Inequality Re-examined.* Oxford: Oxford University Press.

Squire, Lyn. 1993. "Fighting Poverty." *American Economic Review, Papers and Proceedings* 83 (2):377–82.

Thorbecke, Erik. 1991. "Adjustment, Growth, and Income Distribution in Indonesia." *World Development* 19:1595–1614.

Tsiddon, Daniel. 1992. "A Moral Hazard Trap to Growth." *International Economic Review* 33:299–321.

Watkins, Kevin. 1995. *The OXFAM Poverty Report.* Oxford: OXFAM.

World Bank. 1990. *World Development Report.* New York: Oxford University Press.

———. 1991. *Assistance Strategies to Reduce Poverty.* World Bank Policy Paper. Washington, DC: World Bank.

———. 1993. *The East Asian Miracle: Economic Growth and Public Policy.* New York: Oxford University Press.

CHAPTER 4

Stabilization, Adjustment, and Human Development

Lance Taylor

A new socioeconomic environment emerged from the economic dislocations of the late 1970s and early 1980s for both industrialized and developing countries. This chapter concentrates on the latter, reviewing the
policy packages commonly known as "structural adjustment programs"
(or SAPs) and their implications for social welfare and income distribution. The crucial issue is that the recent macroeconomic history of most
poor economies, particularly those of sub-Saharan Africa and Latin
America, is best understood as an ongoing sequence of shocks as opposed to the cyclical ups and downs of external conditions and internal
activity levels characteristic of the first decades after World War II.
SAPs have not been notably successful in coping with this novel economic regime. This macroeconomic history is outlined in the first section, followed by discussions of the social impacts of stabilization and
adjustment and their interactions with human development.

The Historical Record

The basic scenario is that after the relatively high raw materials prices
and low real interest rates of the 1970s, the debt crisis and adverse long-
term trends in the terms of trade sharply cut supplies of hard currency,
especially to Latin American and sub-Saharan African countries, respectively. SAPs began to be applied to deal with balance of payments
problems and associated internal inflationary, distributional, and fiscal
disequilibria.

Almost all programs incorporated a policy mix now widely known
as "neoliberal" or "market friendly," based on a body of economic
doctrine called the "Washington Consensus." SAPs rely on an explicit
sequencing of policies that derives from the historical division of labor
between the International Monetary Fund (IMF) and the World Bank.

The goal is to ensure economic reform in the form of higher output growth and rising real incomes by first "stabilizing" the macroeconomy — the domain of the IMF — and then "adjusting" the market through supply-side reforms — the task of the World Bank. As a synthetic product of the 1980s, the Washington Consensus increasingly appears to be incapable of dealing with many of the difficulties transition and developing economies confront a decade after the market friendly package was cobbled together.

Trade and external capital market pressures were at the root of slow growth and regressive income distribution for many poor economies, both when external resources were scarce (from the late 1970s through the late 1980s) and when (for some countries at least) they became more plentiful thereafter. In the first phase, a difficult stabilization process was unavoidable in most cases because since the establishment of the Bretton Woods system the global macrosystem has been biased toward forcing all corrections to trade imbalances to be made by deficit countries (the United States, at least to date, excluded). To the contractionary, inflationary effects of such adjustments, moreover, destabilizing influences from renewed capital inflows have recently been added.

The debt crisis and adverse trends in the terms of trade sharply cut supplies of hard currency, especially to Latin American and sub-Saharan African countries. An economy can cut back imports to adjust to such a shock in just a few ways. The two most important are contraction of demand "injections," such as investment and fiscal spending, and increases in saving "leakages" through inflationary income and wealth redistributions toward affluent households with high propensities to save. To these can be added devices such as running up external payments arrears, bidding up local interest rates, and shifting the relative price structure toward internationally traded commodities.

Besides slowing growth, economic "stabilization" via these channels tends to make the income distribution more concentrated, increase poverty, and reduce social well-being. Outside East and South Asia, this is the basic macroeconomic story for the 1980s. In Latin America, the initial stabilization crunch came with the debt crisis, when economies were forced to switch from trade deficits of several percentage points of GDP to surpluses of the same magnitude. Capital formation was an important component of the injections curtailed, while inflation took off as a means to increase savings leakages. The price spirals were more dramatic than in other regions because of Latin America's well-established mechanisms for "easing the pain" of (and thereby accelerating) inflation by contract indexation.

At the same time, the outstanding foreign debt was nationalized, meaning that governments had to run large fiscal surpluses apart from external obligations in order to be in a position to service them. Alongside the binding "external gap," this "fiscal gap" played an important role in holding down overall capital formation by cutting back on the historically important phenomenon of "crowding-in" of private by public investment. Countries in which the government received more generous foreign support and/or controlled export proceeds so that it did not have to try to extract them from the private sector did better under the circumstances, for example, Mexico and Chile.

Another sort of problem began to arise in the early 1990s, when several Latin American and other economies began to receive inflows of risk capital and/or direct foreign investment triggered by reductions in interest rates in the OECD and shifts in investor confidence. By choosing not to impose controls on risk capital movements, the authorities in countries like Mexico and Turkey destabilized their economies by linking the inherently volatile markets for internal finance and external capital flows. Other economies in "greater Latin America" such as Argentina, Egypt, India, and the Philippines have thus far avoided financial crises but are being driven toward a high interest rate/strong exchange rate policy mix that is anything but conducive to sustained capital formation and growth.

Problems similar to Latin America's also appeared in the late 1980s and early 1990s in the formerly socialist economies of Eastern Europe when they were subjected to an enormous neoliberal policy shock. The gist was that controls on all markets were suddenly lifted at the same time as the institutional planning structure of socialism was dismantled. The first change meant that aggregate demand rose, while the second curtailed aggregate supply. The resulting excess demand imbalance was similar to that caused by the external shocks discussed above (in Latin America and sub-Saharan Africa the supply reduction was more important, as production had to be cut back because of lack of vital imports). The outcomes were very similar — inflation, output collapses, and regressive income redistributions. Net investment has fallen close to zero, offering dismal prospects for renewed growth in the future. Once again, a policy package strongly supported by existing world and local institutions and political forces had socially disastrous results.

The plight of sub-Saharan Africa is even worse than those of Eastern Europe and Latin America — for almost 20 years only a handful of more than 40 economies have experienced periods of positive per capita income growth. The region has been under intensive SAP treatment for more than a decade, with minimal returns even though many countries are receiving capital inflows on the order of 10 percent of GDP (not a large sum in absolute terms for a nation with, say, 5 million people and a per capita income of U.S.$300).

No one has a clear solution for Africa's weak economic performance. "Surplus extraction" from export agriculture to benefit urban-based industrialization was an important element of the region's development strategies after World War II. Although there were substantial internal resource transfers, several factors intervened to make the strategy unsuccessful.

Externally, trends in the export terms of trade for the food, beverage, fiber, and mineral exports it produces were consistently unfavorable. Internally, lack of investment in infrastructure and technological improvement hampered agricultural output growth while industrial strategies did not bear fruit. More recently, there have been continuing adverse shifts in the terms of trade, escalating interest obligations on its external debt, and donor proliferation. On the latter count, a typical finance minister might go to the airport 300 times a year to meet visiting dignitaries. She or he has much more pressing things to do!

On the plate of market friendliness, however, several unsavory morsels rest. First, if neoliberal policies take an extended period of time to work in places like Chile and fall apart in Mexico and Turkey, what is their promise for Africa? At that moment, African "success" cases like Ghana and Uganda are basically being kept afloat for demonstration purposes by continuing aid inflows. They finance intermediate imports to keep production going as well as providing a sizable demand injection from a new "four-wheel drive class" of foreign advisers and their families, who have spread across the continent. These incoming loans are piling up substantial interest obligations for the future. Unless very recent efforts toward forgiveness on the part of the World Bank bear fruit, a repayment crisis for official debt will loom.

Second, until recently the World Bank pushed all African countries to expand their primary product exports, even though an enhanced global supply of such commodities is bound to drive down their prices. An easy alternative would be to put resources into schemes via which collaborating national commodity producers could regulate and restrain supply to stabilize prices at "reasonable" levels, although Washington's current principles may preclude it.

Finally, as we will see in discussing East Asia, concerted state intervention in those economies was an essential part of their development strategies. Such an approach might well be inappropriate in Africa for a variety of reasons. However, the degree of IMF and World Bank control in the region is so great that no nation would be permitted to attempt the Asian model even if a democratically chosen national leadership wanted to try it.

In contrast to most countries in the other poor regions, economies in East and South Asia passed through the period 1975–95 in relatively robust condition. A complete explanation of their success remains to be provided, but the important facts are that they did not run up large external obligations in the 1970s (partly because of prudent policy and partly because most Asian countries were not as subject as Latin America or Nigeria to loan pushing by commercial banks) and they had diversified their exports toward manufacturing and so were not as strongly hit as sub-Saharan Africa by declining raw material export prices after 1977. Their favorable foreign exchange positions and relatively high savings rates permitted reasonably (or strongly, as in China and India) expansionary fiscal policies to be pursued.

In Southeast Asia, Malaysia, Indonesia, and Thailand also maintained controls on capital movements and practiced aggressive industrial policies. In the wake of the exchange rate realignments of the mid-1980s, they began to receive big inflows of direct foreign investment from the "first tier" of Asian industrializers (Japan, South Korea, and Taiwan). Their regulated capital markets enabled the Southeast Asian economies to channel foreign capital toward physical capital formation in export sectors. High domestic saving rates could support this process as opposed to holding down aggregate demand and spilling over into capital flight because the impetus to invest was there.

The distributional effects of these changes have differed among countries. The "head count ratio," or share of the population in poverty, fell in most of Asia in response to steady output growth. On the other hand, the income distribution on a class/sector or size basis became more concentrated in nations such as Thailand (greater Bangkok versus the rest of the country) and China (the booming South versus lagging regions). How increasing relative inequality in previously egalitarian societies will feed into the political equation remains to be seen.

Social Impacts of Stabilization

The literature attempting to assess the social impacts of structural adjustment packages is plentiful, and the tenor of individual contributions ranges widely. One immediate implication is that it is impossible to trace the effects of programs in the absence of a coherent theoretical framework and (equally important) a deep knowledge of the institutional and sociopolitical structure of an economy to which a SAP is being applied. A structuralist framework helps illuminate microlevel findings regarding the interactions of SAPs with gender relations, the environment, health, and education.

Similar to the behavior of income distribution and poverty indicators, one main finding is that the absence of a significant deterioration in

a particular social indicator during periods of structural adjustment —
such as, for example, mortality rates or female poverty incidence —
should not automatically be equated with the absence of negative overall
effects.

For instance, poverty is reflected in many indicators beyond head
count ratios, including the degree of poverty; depletion of physical,
financial, and natural resource stocks; and access to social services. It
would therefore be plausible to argue for negative poverty consequences
of structural adjustment without an observed upswing of poverty incidence. There is ample anecdotal evidence, particularly for sub-Saharan
Africa, hinting that IMF-style austerity programs actually worsen the
welfare position of the poor.

Positive or negative effects from the environment and social sectors
such as health, education, and gender relations feeding back onto macroeconomic performance are to be expected. But the interactions between
stabilization, adjustment, growth, and human development are complex
and not entirely understood. Figure 4.1 illustrates some possibilities that
arise.

Beginning at the bottom, the diagram shows that stabilization itself
involves a complex set of maneuvers. Experience suggests, first, that
overall macroeconomic stability cannot be assured unless the financial
balances of the fiscal, foreign, monetary, and private sectors are not
excessively in deficit or surplus. Three recent examples underline the
point.

By the early 1990s, Mexico had done everything that orthodoxy
recommends in terms of fiscal and monetary adjustment — the fiscal account was in surplus and there was adequate monetary control. Yet the
foreign account was heavily in deficit because private savings had collapsed and hot money was flowing in. All that an IMF-style stabilizer
could try to do to overcome the problem was increase the fiscal surplus
(cutting back still more on capital formation and capacity growth), raise
interest rates (bringing more short-term external capital in), or devalue
(causing external funds already in the country to stampede out because of
a capital loss, as finally occurred in Mexico). In effect, an "adjustment" or
"structural" problem of excessively high import demand derailed an orthodox stabilization attempt. In the Mexican case, the root causes were
rapid import liberalization, an overvalued exchange rate, and ultimately
lack of confidence on the part of the private sector in the durability of the
program.

Second, Russia's current predicament suggests that even if Central
Bank interventions overcome one set of difficulties they can worsen
others. In a "payments crisis" in 1992, there was a huge buildup in inter-
enterprise arrears as firms continued to sell to one another when the

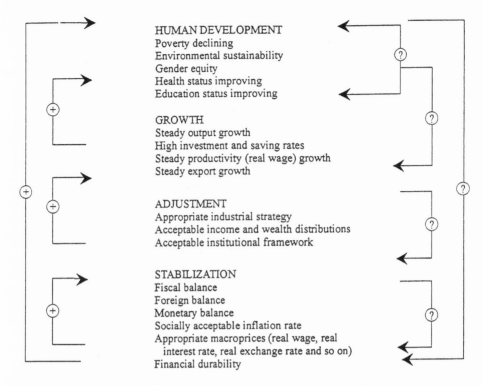

Fig. 4.1. Stabilization, adjustment, growth, and human development

authorities attempted to restrain credit. To prevent a wave of bankrupt-
cies, these delayed payments were ultimately taken over by the Central
Bank, which also lent massively to finance the government's deficit.
These loans or increases in the bank's asset portfolio had to be offset by
increased liabilities in the form of money emission and a buildup in
commercial bank excess deposit reserves. The commercial banks, in
turn, are unable to lend because household and enterprise savings flows
remain high while investment has collapsed. The savings surplus spills
over into capital flight. This web of financial imbalances is not likely to
promote real output growth even though ample "resources" in the form
of private savings and foreign capital inflows are at hand.

Finally, as SAPs went into action in the early 1980s, the poor,
primary exporting countries in sub-Saharan Africa and elsewhere began
to receive additional foreign assistance to "compensate" for continuing
decreases in export prices and rising (official) debt burdens. The inflow
of hard currency covered two big deficits — the excess of imports over

exports and of government outlays over revenues. Because there were few legal channels through which the foreign aid could be absorbed by a private sector deficit or excess of investment over saving (as in Mexico), the public sector was forced into the red.

Even apart from dealing with donors' diverse forms of aid conditionality, coping with such largesse is difficult. To borrow a metaphor from the conservative Austrian economists Menger and Hayek, foreign import support does not enter an economy "organically" as an internally generated income flow; the ways in which it is received and spent by the government can upset the macrosystem. For example, external assistance may help raise the levels of economic activity and investment, but these favorable changes (especially the latter) are unlikely to occur without an active private sector receiving directed public support. Some of the extra foreign exchange will spill over into higher private incomes (perhaps illegally) and certainly into increased imports or reduced exports. There is always a risk of capital flight or (especially in Africa or Russia for that matter) smuggling, which has the effects of increasing the "official" trade deficit and facilitating a transfer of foreign inflows to the private sector. All these changes represent a diversion of the national savings effort — a poor omen for future growth.

These three disequilibrium situations illustrate a common theme: there are positive feedbacks across financial balances. If one is badly out of line, then overall macroaccounting forces others to be disequilibrated in a vicious circle. On the contrary, in a virtuous circle financial equilibrium in one part of the economy stimulates it in others. Such "lose-lose" or "win-win" scenarios carry over into other aspects of stabilization and adjustment as well.

"Excessive" money creation is known to be associated with socially or politically unacceptable rates of inflation. But inflation can also be triggered by social conflict over the division of the national "pie," that is, the existing income and wealth distributions have to be acceptable to the citizenry at large (as noted under the "Adjustment" heading in fig. 4.1). And, as already noted, by means of forced saving and inflationary tax mechanisms, rapidly rising prices lead to further income concentration and potential unrest.

"Macroprices" have to be in line with social and productive limitations on economic performance. A very strong or "overvalued" real exchange rate represents an external disaster in the making, as it stimulates imports and holds down exports. A high real interest rate strangles investment demand and (in the absence of capital controls) draws in speculative foreign finance. An excessively high real wage can hold down exports, and an excessively low one can provoke social conflict and/or inflation.

Financial fragility, especially in the context of unregulated external capital movements, can lead to macroeconomic disaster. Financial "durability," assured by sensible regulation and appropriate private sector behavioral norms, feeds back fruitfully into other parts of a stabilization effort.

Adjustment

The possibility of vicious and virtuous circles carries over into adjustment, as is illustrated by the arrows in figure 4.1. A crucial point (illustrated strikingly by Chile's experience in the 1980s) is that adjustment may be impossible without stabilization and vice versa. But adjustment cannot occur unless other factors are favorable as well.

First, sustained output growth per capita has to be supported by relatively high investment rates in physical capital formation and/or increases in productivity per worker (and perhaps per unit of capital as well). The investment can only be financed successfully over the long run if national savings rates are correspondingly high. Because labor productivity growth puts workers out of jobs, it can retard aggregate demand. Either real wages must increase to permit more real consumer spending or exports must rise to absorb the extra potential output made possible by productivity growth.

How these beneficial developments can be assured remains very much an open question, as is illustrated by the contrasts drawn in the East Asian context between the "market friendly" approach and the more directed industrial strategy that those countries pursued. (Of course, a state-backed "agricultural" strategy could be appropriate in some circumstances, as in Chile over the decades following World War II.)

It is also clear that "adjustment" to stable, long-run growth will not occur if there is acute or even latent distributional tension. Moreover, the entire institutional framework conditions the possibilities for growth. Adequate institutions and acceptable distribution tend to support high investment and productivity growth. Export expansion and productivity gains are unlikely without solid public sector backing, which is not possible without macroeconomic stability. Again, we are in a positive feedback regime.

Human Development

Although outside "Washington" there is no consensus about how macroeconomic stability and adjustment can be attained, the points of disagreement are relatively clear. The same cannot be (fully) said about linkages between macroeconomics and human development. Some positive feedback is certainly present among the elements of human well-being listed at the top of figure 4.1 and within the economic system. By means of "trickle down," faster output growth can alleviate poverty and intensive environmental exploitation. Accumulation of human capital in the form of better health and more education is at least a necessary condition for faster productivity growth. However, the signs of other effects are less clear.

First, does greater equity stimulate output and growth in the short to medium run? On the one hand, recent research in this area suggests that developing economies may be "wage led," in that high payments to labor stimulate aggregate demand, while the opposite is true in industrialized parts of the world. On the other hand, industrial country evidence suggests that specific policies such as the provision of public goods (education, training, communications, transport) and the mitigation of public, capitalist, and worker conflicts can reduce a "full employment profit squeeze" on capital accumulation and thus promote faster potential output growth at higher levels of capacity utilization. These considerations are at the heart of the structuralist macromodel sketched in the next section and underlie the ambiguous feedback arrows running from the human development area of figure 4.1.

Second, research has yet to isolate clear linkages among, say, improved gender equity, environmental improvements, and economic performance. Insofar as changes in these indicators are seen as side effects of macrodevelopments without well-defined feedback to the economic system, they are not likely to be given much weight in "hard-headed" policy discussions.

Third, many green activists and researchers see output (and population) growth as being extremely damaging to the environment; economists tend to think the other way. The signs of many potentially important effects remain to be determined and may be worked out only over decades- or centuries-long time spans.

Fourth, interactions among all of figure 4.1's human development indicators are complex. On the whole, the typical effect of one on another may well be positive, but exceptions are easy to imagine.

Finally, if positive linkages dominate, the virtuous circles or "win-win" scenarios they can support are pleasant to contemplate. But there is an ever-present risk that under certain circumstances they can give rise to vicious circles or even a "lose-lose" socioeconomic/environmental crash. A particularly damaging example of such positive feedback is environmental degradation induced by and further inducing extreme poverty.

Equity (E)

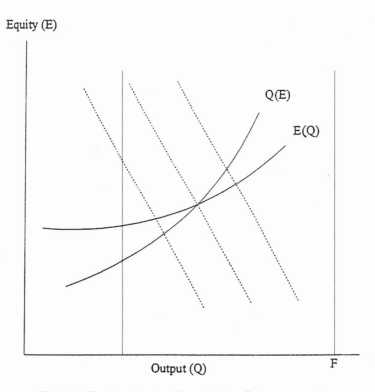

Output (Q)   F

Fig. 4.2.   Equity and output in a structuralist macromodel

Structuralist Macroeconomics

It makes sense to restate the ideas underlying the foregoing discussion in a somewhat more formal fashion; this will also help focus ideas in the policy discussion below. Two diagrams commonly used in structuralist macroeconomic analysis illustrate the issues that arise.

Figure 4.2 is the first diagram. "Equity" E runs along the vertical axis, indicated by a high real wage, low Gini coefficient, and so on. Output Q appears on the horizontal axis, but it is bounded above by F, the level of "full capacity" or potential output feasible at any time. Growth of F is assumed to depend on investment I in human and/or physical capital, and it can be assumed that I responds positively to both Q and E. Finally, actual output can lie below its potential, that is, full employment of productive resources is not presupposed (contrary to most orthodox models).

The diagram shows the "wage-led" case mentioned earlier. Output in an unconstrained macroequilibrium responds positively to increased equity along the Q(E) schedule. The positive slope characterizes developing economies; a negative slope is more typical in industrialized countries where exports and investment are cut back as labor costs rise. Due to "trickle down," the fact that real wages respond positively to the level of economic activity, and similar channels, there is also likely to be a positive effect of output on equity, as indicated in the E(Q) schedule. Finally, the dashed lines are members of a set of growth rate contour lines or iso-investment loci, each one showing combinations of Q and E that give rise to a constant level of I. Higher investment and faster potential output growth correspond to a dashed line further to the northeast.

Now suppose that output is suddenly limited to a level, $\bar{Q}$, which lies below initial full capacity F and is also less than the output level corresponding to an initial macroeconomic equilibrium where the solid curves cross. As is shown in figure 4.2, such a limit could reflect a foreign exchange dearth of the sort that affected Latin America and sub-Saharan Africa in the 1980s. Another possibility is that a capacity constraint can suddenly bind as demand surges (transitorily) up and potential output down, as they did after market decontrol in Eastern Europe. Somehow, this new restriction on Q must be satisfied.

One way for Q to reach $\bar{Q}$ is via a leftward shift of the Q(E) curve as demand injections fall and leakages rise — the adjustment mechanisms discussed previously. The lower consumption demand or higher saving behind this shift usually requires an inflationary income and wealth transfer toward the wealthy, so that the E(Q) curve slides down as well. The directions in which the schedules move suggest that a new, stagnant equilibrium can emerge to the left of Q, as may be the case in sub-Saharan Africa and Eastern Europe. Potential output growth will also slow, as investment falls toward the southwest through the family of dashed contour lines.

If leftward and downward movements of the schedules reflect changes in nonindustrialized economies outside South and East Asia, the opposite is true for those favored regions. Export and investment expansions have shifted Q(E) to the right, while E(Q) has kept its original position or at least not shifted radically downward. How policy interventions can help sustain the Asian situation and propel the rest of the developing and postsocialist worlds in its direction is a topic for the following section.

Before getting into such issues, however, it makes sense to explore more fully how developing economies can adjust to external shocks. A "three-gap" model, as is illustrated in figure 4.3, helps describe the possibilities. The growth rate *g* of potential output F is measured on the

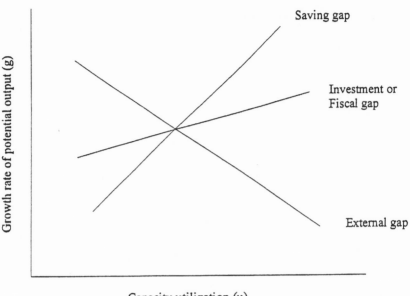

Fig. 4.3. A three-gap model

vertical axis, while capacity utilization $u = Q/F$ appears on the horizontal. There are three crucial relationships among these variables.

The first is imposed by the need for external balance. In a developing country, more economic activity typically draws in intermediate and other forms of imports, while it may cut back on export sales. At the same time, the import content of gross capital formation is high. Hence, for a given trade deficit (sustained, e.g., by new private or public capital inflows net of interest payments abroad) there is an inverse tradeoff between u and g. If one variable goes up, the other must decline, as illustrated by the "external gap" schedule in the diagram. This curve will shift in response to several key variables. In many countries, it moved sharply downward at the onset of the debt crisis in 1982 and began to slide back up in the late 1980s when private capital flows became more plentiful. As already discussed, both such shifts may be difficult to absorb.

Investment is also limited by available saving, which on Keynesian grounds can be assumed to be an increasing function of the level of economic activity. This relationship underlies the upward-sloping "saving gap" schedule. Its position can shift in response to a variety of forces. In Mexico, for example, the national saving rate fell by around 10 percent of GDP in the early 1990s as rapid trade liberalization and exchange overvaluation led households and firms to buy enthusiastically abroad. Such conversion of an escalating trade deficit into consumption as opposed to capital formation did not bode well for future growth — even before the financial collapse of December 1994.

Another macroeconomic variable affecting saving behavior is inflation. More rapid price increases are likely to shift the schedule upward via "forced saving" (income redistribution against low-saving classes such as wage earners whose incomes are not fully indexed to more rapidly rising prices) and the "inflation tax" (erosion of wealth by inflation, which leads asset holders to save more to compensate for capital losses). These modes of macroadjustment were central features of many countries' reactions to the 1982 debt shock.

Finally, investment itself may be spurred by higher capacity utilization of the traditional accelerator. In a somewhat more roundabout, though empirically relevant, process, private capital formation may respond to (or be "crowded" by) public investment, especially in infrastructure. If fiscal revenues net of current expenditures rise as a function of u, then so can the sum of public and (crowded) private levels of investment. These two mechanisms give rise to the positively sloped "investment or fiscal gap."

Improvements in fiscal positions have been one positive outcome of orthodox adjustment packages implemented in Latin America and to some extent elsewhere (although revenue gains due to privatization of state enterprises will prove to be transitory). On the contrary, India's growth spurt in the 1980s was associated with increasing ratios of fiscal and external debts to GDP as restrictions that had been binding in previous decades started to loosen. There was a sudden crunch in 1991, but foreign capital flowed in again following liberalization maneuvers. Whether fiscal and external constraints on Indian growth will shift downward remains to be seen. Renewed increases in debt ratios are not a good omen.

Capital formation itself is tricky to manage. With state guidance, China has been finding investment outlets for its massive capital inflows and domestic savings supply (in light of the experience of Mexico and Turkey, of course, there is no reason to expect the inflow of funds to persist indefinitely). Other countries appear to be investment constrained. Russia, in particular, has suffered an enormous investment collapse in the wake of the disintegration of its socialist planning system.

These examples suggest that the gap framework can be used in various ways. One takes the form of ex post decompositions of shifts in the schedules. Another is a discussion of which constraint(s) may be predetermined, with the others adjusting their position(s) via endogenous variable shifts. Identification of such "binding" gap(s) in different time periods is an approach often adopted by practitioners, in part drawing upon political economy considerations.

The behavioral content of the simple model in figure 4.3 can easily be enriched. For example, one obvious question is how macroprice changes such as real devaluation or real wage cuts underlie movements in the schedules under different hypotheses about binding constraints. In a macro-micro linkage, will rural credit restrictions and higher interest rates under a binding saving constraint force poor farmers toward land-intensive, environmentally degrading, agricultural practices? Finally, the model can be extended to deal with dynamic relationships between external capital movements and growth.

More Rational Policy

A full set of alternatives to the Washington Consensus remains to be created, and it may never be. The diversity of developing and post-socialist countries' institutional and historical experiences rules out any uniformly applicable policy mix; as the recent Eastern European experience shows, no country is a tabula rasa waiting to be imprinted with industrial capitalism. Moreover, there is no very strong tradition of doing macroeconomics as if poor people and social processes mattered. Much remains to be discovered, but at the moment some policy proposals can still be made.

First, adjusting to difficulties such as a tightened external constraint, an overvalued exchange rate, or a set of disequilibrated macroeconomic balances almost always carries social costs. Depending on the way in which the economic system functions, different social groups will bear the burdens; the weak and poor are in particular danger of being hurt. Directed "meso" policies can help offset this problem, but its resolution ultimately requires systemic change. With regard to meso policies, it is also worth emphasizing that in many cases they are second-order corrections to first-order macrodislocations such as output fluctuations of tens of percentage points and percentage shifts of equal or greater magnitude in "macroprices" like the real wage or real exchange rate. The greater gain in social equity comes from avoiding such wrenching shocks.

Second, for many countries an external constraint in the form of poor export prices or a heavy debt burden appears to have become a quasi-permanent condition. The three-gap model illustrates how by easing the resulting import compression ample capital inflows can facilitate the adjustment process, but they are by no means a sufficient condition. Much depends on how effectively external resources are utilized. Mexico's huge injections of foreign private money in the 1990s, for example, were used to "finance" a reduction of the private saving rate of about 10 percent of GDP in a liberalized market environment. In terms of figure 4.3, the saving gap schedule shifted downward to offset the potential increment in the growth rate permitted by an upward movement of the external gap. In much of sub-Saharan Africa, official assistance similarly underwrites public consumption and unproductive transfers to the private sector. Unless "foreign saving" entering a national economy via its trade deficit is effectively transformed into capital formation, it causes long-term harm. In historically successful national transitions to sustained output growth, the state played a key role in this intermediation process.

Third, industrial strategy involving trade protection; financial market control; corporatist deals among the state, capital, and labor; and other nonliberal interventions has been associated with rapid growth in South Korea and all other successful capitalist economies (the United States before World War II, continental Europe after 1945, and Japan, Brazil, and the countries of Southeast Asia over various time periods). Many scholars see direct causal links, although their strength depends crucially on such country characteristics as size, natural resource endowment, human capital base, and prevailing sociopolitical relationships.

Fourth, an implied policy question is how to invent appropriate "macro-micro" policy linkages, for example, coordination of macroeconomic, industrial, and educational policy along South Korean lines or design of programs to minimize and ameliorate the social costs of contractionary, inflationary, macroeconomic adjustments. In light of each country's own distributional dynamics, how can social programs most effectively be deployed?

Fifth, social support in the form of the provision of education and health services as well as targeted income redistribution has also been associated with growth under appropriate conditions. Before 1977, Sri Lanka grew slowly in spite its well-developed human resource base. Thereafter, it grew steadily when import strangulation was removed by official external support. Subject to such caveats, scholars discern direct causality from human capital accumulation and other forms of social investment to output growth and greater equity. Their effective programming is a pressing policy task.

Sixth, linkages of gender equity, environmental quality, and similar variables to output growth are important now and will be more so in the future. These indicators do not correlate totally with social equity, as is indicated by widespread environmental stress in Sri Lanka and India's Kerala State and South Korea's labor repression and low wage rates for women, but subtle connections certainly do exist. How they can be made to feed into "win-win" virtuous circles as opposed to "lose-lose" vicious ones is a problem that all countries confront.

Seventh, whether environmental improvements and sustained output (and population) growth are mutually consistent is very much an open question. Some economists believe that accumulation processes for physical, human, and natural capital can trade off in a harmonious fashion; environmental activists and researchers think not. Environmentally friendly policies will certainly involve shifts in prevailing consumption and production patterns, but no one has a clear idea about how they are to be created.

Eighth, gradualism in adjustment and stable capital movements can help ease the pain of macroeconomic shocks. In the absence of systemic reforms such as internationally imposed controls (or "Tobin taxes") on capital movements, countries can themselves act to restrain capital inflows (as was done recently in Colombia and Chile) and build up non-monetized external holdings when the terms of trade improve (as they may now be doing). Many features of the international economic system are rigged to favor rich economies, and they have a vested interest in maintaining the status quo. But that does not mean that poor countries are powerless to protect their interests. Together and separately, they can manage international trade and capital flows to their own benefit. In designing appropriate policies, the precepts of neoliberalism and the Washington Consensus are often best ignored.

Finally, if history suggests that no economies developed without developmentalist states, then states have to transform themselves to that end and be accountable for their reforms. In many (if not most) low- and middle-income nations, restructuring the state will be no easy task. But there will be no real development until it is done.

Directions for Research

Several potentially important research topics have just been mentioned. Others are implicit in the previous discussion. One way to address them would be through a coordinated set of country studies drawing on historical experience and informed by models like those sketched earlier. A possible set of questions to be addressed in a set of studies emphasizing new policy directions for the future could include the following.

First, throughout Latin America, Africa, and Eastern Europe there are clear tendencies for poverty to increase and the income and wealth distributions to become more concentrated related to macro–price shifts and also to slow growth caused by the debt crisis and market liberalization programs that failed. Now that capital is (for the moment, at least) flowing into some countries, how can it be used to underwrite not just growth but equitable growth? An analytical framework like the one illustrated in figures 4.2 and 4.3 is required to address such a question and should be agreed upon by country researchers before their studies begin.

Second, as we have seen, in the design of industrial and agricultural policy, "micro-macro" coordination issues remain unresolved. Experience over the past two decades shows that liberalization is not a sufficient condition for efficiency gains. There is no history under capitalism of completely unrestricted markets and much evidence that collaboration among large economic actors is central to output and productivity growth. In the context of a given country's institutions and income distribution, how can it be attained?

Third, Mexico's and Turkey's recent histories show how attempts to implant market friendly policies can lead rapidly to macroeconomic instability (as indeed the Southern Cone experience of the late 1970s has already shown). Ways to open economies while avoiding highly destabilizing capital movements remain to be discovered. Saving rates have to be increased, while at the same time outlets for saving in the form of productive investment projects have to be provided.

Fourth, a growing problem not caused by recent macropolicy developments is environmental degradation. Recent estimates put environmental costs in the range of several percentage points of GDP — a level at which they become macroeconomically important. Potential dynamic repercussions of the type discussed earlier are not easy to think about concretely (let alone model formally), but they cry out to be examined.

Social equity, saving, investment, micro-macro issues, instability, and environmental problems comprise an ample menu for any study group to consider. Nonetheless, an effort by open but experienced minds to explore these themes could have big potential payoffs in both the short and long runs, not least in setting up an agenda to be pursued by independently minded researchers. Their results could also feed into a renewed discussion of the goals of development aid.

Ultimately, the United Nations system itself might assume a greater voice in the formulation of alternative policy designs. This issue at times appears to be unduly "academic," and macroeconomics is undeniably abstract. Nonetheless, it has enormous practical impacts (e.g., about 50 million people in Eastern Europe now live in poverty because present and former academic economists persuaded political leaders to adopt policies based upon "global shocks"). A network of economists with practical experience in formulating policy in developing and postsocialist economies could help offset such biases and provide the intellectual firepower needed to formulate policy packages more appropriate than the Washington blend.

CHAPTER 5

Fiscal Policy and Income Distribution

Vito Tanzi

In 1974, I wrote an article published in Banca Nazionale del Lavoro's *Quarterly Review* on "Redistributing Income through the Budget in Latin America," which discussed the role of fiscal policy in redistributing income. Since then, issues surrounding income distribution have been attracting the attention of academics and policymakers alike, and the IMF even organized a conference on income distribution and sustainable growth in 1995.

In principle, fiscal policy provides the necessary tools to redistribute income and protect the poor and the disadvantaged in line with society's perception of justice and equality. However, there tends to be a gap between the normative role assigned to government and its actual ability to do so. Experience has shown that government policies have often failed to generate the intended effect on income distribution or poverty, and relatively more affluent groups have tended to benefit from various government programs. I will also argue that complementing stabilization programs with structural reforms to improve the economy's allocative efficiency and create conditions for sustainable growth can have significant negative effects on income distribution in the short term.

Budgetary policies *can* play an important role in redistributing income. A properly designed system of taxation can theoretically change relative incomes in a society. That is, the tax system can be made sufficiently progressive so that the after-tax distribution of income is closer to that deemed desirable by society. In practice, however, this may be difficult to achieve for both administrative and political reasons (I will turn to them later). At the same time, it needs to be recognized that in Latin America a mere change in relative incomes is not enough given the depth of poverty. It is also necessary to ensure that the poorest groups receive at least the absolute minimum. This is where public expenditure has a contribution to make, especially in the areas of health, education, and transfer programs.

In principle, social spending can have a positive effect on income distribution (and growth) if it is accomplished in an efficient manner and the benefits actually accrue to the poor. However, I will argue (as I did over 25 years ago) that the capture of benefits by the urban middle classes (be it directly or indirectly through government jobs) has prevented significant changes in income distribution, especially in Latin America. Second, I will argue that the protection of social expenditure under structural adjustment is also a worthwhile cause in principle, but only if social programs are targeted to the poor. Otherwise, protecting social expenditure and expanding social safety nets become the protection of vested interests in disguise.

Budgetary Policies and the Poor

Most empirical studies confirm that the tax systems of Latin America have done little to modify existing income distributions. This is because tax burdens are generally not very heavy in most countries and indirect taxes typically predominate. Income taxes are mostly levied on civil servants and employees of large enterprises. Tax evasion by other groups with similar income levels has undermined the redistributive power of income taxation and also impinged on horizontal equity. There is thus a high dispersion of individual taxpayers around average tax rates. Some taxpayers pay very low taxes, while others who cannot escape the tax net end up paying substantially more than the estimated average tax. Wealth, inheritance, and land taxes can modify income distribution by reducing the income-earning capacity of those who own wealth, but their applicability is very limited. It would be utopian to expect that these taxes will bring about a major change in income distribution in Latin America, although this is not to say that the governments of the Latin American countries should not seek to improve their tax systems by making them more efficient, elastic, and equitable. The evidence from the 1960s shows that taxation had only a marginal impact on the income share of the rich in selected Latin American countries (table 5.1, cols. 1 and 2). It improved the relative income share of the poorest 50 percent of the population by about 0.5 percent. And this was a time when tax systems tended to be more progressive than they are today.

In order to assess and improve the impact of social expenditure on the poor, one needs to know who the poor are and what characterizes them. The poor in Latin America comprise the rural agricultural population with large families and (now much more so than 30 years ago) the urban population inhabiting the slums around the big cities. These groups are typically young and poorly educated. However, it is not only the differences in endowment of physical and human capital that marginalizes the poor; social and ethnic differences and the use of different languages by portions of the rural population often hamper their integration into political life and the economy. In fact, rural subsistence farmers with large families and little education are often not much affected by government policies.

How, then, can the poor benefit from social expenditure? If the poor are mainly young and uneducated, as they tend to be in many Latin American countries, expenditure on child care and nutrition programs, basic health, or primary education would improve the situation of the poor the most. If nutrition, health, and education levels constrain output, such policies would also stimulate economic growth. If the poor are mainly old, health expenditure might be most beneficial. Both situations would seem to provide an obvious argument for increasing social expenditure. However, the first type of expenditure (focused on the young) can be seen as an investment, while the second has to be seen as pure consumption.

Social Expenditure and Income Distribution in the 1960s

Reality unfortunately is much different from the ideal policies advocated by economists and policymakers. As early as the 1960s, it was not the poorest 20 percent of the population who were benefiting from social expenditure programs as much as the middle classes. Table 5.1 illustrates the impact of social expenditure on income distribution in selected Latin American countries (cols. 2–4). What emerges is that, as a consequence of education spending, the relative income share of the poorer half of the population improved by 0.6 percent in Colombia. The impact of all

TABLE 5.1.   Income Share of Population Segments: Latin America, 1960s

	Before Tax (1)	After Tax (2)	Including Benefits from Social Expenditure (3)	Change in Income Share from Expenditure Only (4)
		Income share of poorest 50 percent		
Colombia	13.5	13.9	14.5[a]	+0.6
Mexico	19.0	20.6	21.9	+1.3
Argentina	23.4	23.9	25.9	+2.0
		Income share of poorest 20 percent		
Mexico	5.8	6.1	6.9	+0.8
Argentina	7.0	7.7	8.3	+0.6

Source: Tanzi 1974.

[a] Benefits from education expenditure only.

social spending was to raise the relative income share of the same population segment by 1.3 percent in Mexico and 2 percent in Argentina. The income share of the poorest quintile in Mexico and Argentina increased by less than 1 percent as a result of this spending by their governments. It seems that the third to fifth income deciles improved their relative share of income more than the poorest quintile in these two countries. In many Latin American countries, government policies had a significant positive impact on the incomes of the upper middle classes. In Mexico, for example, it was the top 5 to 20 percent income group that benefited the most from public expenditure by increasing its relative income share by 3.1 percent.

These numbers, however, underestimate the bias in the allocation of benefits from public spending. Public expenditures in Latin America typically tend to be concentrated in urban areas and richer regions, where, for example, schools and hospitals are more concentrated and better equipped. In the rural areas and poorer regions, schools are more crowded and of poorer quality and health centers and hospitals are more scarce, so that the poor are likely to benefit the least from social expenditure. If the poor are also segregated via ethnic, language, and cultural barriers, this leads to a further lowering of the benefits from public expenditure and a worsening of their relative income position.

The comparison of school retention rates between rural and urban areas further illustrates the extent of the bias. For instance, the retention rates in urban areas of Colombia, the Dominican Republic, Guatemala, and Panama were between 47 and 80 percent in the 1960s. By contrast, the retention rate in rural areas in these countries ranged between 3.5 and 45 percent. And what "benefit" does a child receive when he or she drops out of primary school after a few years with no major impact on his or her future economic opportunities?

It seems that redistribution in the 1960s largely involved a transfer of wealth from the very rich to those who were not poor. The rich generally pay higher taxes, but they were likely to send their children to private schools and use private health facilities. They do not hold public sector jobs, except probably the top positions. Members of the urban middle class, on the other hand, benefit the most from social expenditure since they rely on public schools and hospitals. Further, budget-financed higher education enables them to secure civil service jobs. This led me to conclude that "it is very unlikely that increasing public expenditure will bring about a better distribution of income unless such an expenditure is provided with a degree of selectivity, which does not seem possible under present Latin American conditions" (Tanzi 1974, 81).

Social Expenditure in the 1980s and 1990s

In recent years, numerous new studies have analyzed the links between public expenditure and income distribution and public expenditure and growth, motivated in part by the recent experiences of different country groups, including Latin America. One fact that has changed in Latin America compared to 30 years ago is increased urbanization, which itself is partly the result of the past pro-urban bias in public expenditure. The number of poor living in urban areas now poses new challenges for the governments in this region.

Some recent studies show that public expenditure in some countries has improved income distribution. For example, Deininger and Squire in a recent cross-country study find that an increase in expenditure on schooling has increased the income share of the bottom quintile and (to a somewhat lesser extent) of the middle class.[1] Public investment expenditure had no such effect.

Other recent studies for Latin America suggest that not much has changed compared to the 1960s. Petrei (1987, 1995) assessed the impact of social expenditure and income distribution in five Latin American countries in 1980 and around 1990. His results are similar to what I found 25 years ago. Table 5.2 shows Petrei's results.

The impact of total social expenditure (defined to include education, health, social security, public housing, and sanitation and water) was "neutral" or slightly regressive for the poorest 20 percent in Argentina, Costa Rica, Chile, the Dominican Republic, and Uruguay. Abstracting from the above-mentioned biases, public expenditure on *primary* education was found to be progressive in all countries except for the Dominican Republic, and benefits from health expenditure seem to have accrued to a large extent to the poor in all countries. The incidence of public expenditure on social security, water and sanitation, housing (except in Argentina), and tertiary education (except in Chile), however, was very regressive. Petrei (1995) also finds that household transfers provided a significant income supplement to poor households, although in absolute terms they received less than the upper income brackets. In the aggregate, between 25 and 30 percent of benefits from social expenditure seem to be accruing to the top quintile of the population in these countries. These results, compared with the probable proportionality of the tax system, raise questions about the overall impact of the public sector on income distribution.

It is interesting to compare the results of 1980 with those of 1990. In Argentina and Costa Rica, the share of benefits accruing to the poorest 20 percent declined during this period. On the other hand, in Chile and Uruguay the "targeting" of social expenditure has improved considerably,

TABLE 5.2. Benefit Incidence of Social Expenditure on the Lowest Quintile in Selected Latin American Countries, 1980–93

	Argentina		Costa Rica		Chile		Dominican Republic	Uruguay	
	1980	1993	1980	1986	1980	1990	1980	1980	1989
Total social expenditure	20.0	17.8	20.9	17.6	14.9	18.8	20.0	15.7	19.6
Total education	28.3	28.6	19.9	15.7	25.8	31.0	10.6	31.4	32.9
Primary	39.9	37.0	34.7	30.0	36.7	35.7	14.2	45.0	51.6
Secondary	26.4	22.0	18.6	17.8	21.0	26.8	9.4	24.7	30.3
Tertiary	8.3	8.3	4.1	1.7	5.5	22.8	—	7.2	5.4
Health	51.2	53.2	30.0	27.7	22.3	24.5	41.3	34.0	34.8
Social security	9.9	5.1	9.3	7.1	6.2	5.7	8.6	10.3	12.4
Public housing	72.7	20.4	5.3	—	42.8	16.5	2.7	7.0	15.7
Water and sanitation	16.0	25.0	17.4	—	14.6	—	8.8	18.0	10.7

Source: Petrei 1987, 1995.

especially in health and education. This shows that explicit attention paid to equity by policymakers can improve the impact of fiscal policy on income distribution.

Recent data for Brazil also indicate that there is inefficiency in social expenditures that largely benefit the nonpoor. Total expenditure on public education (4.2 percent of GDP in 1990) is quite high, but almost one-quarter is spent on tertiary education. Another quarter of education expenditure is allocated to "administration," probably providing low-productivity jobs to the middle class. In Brazil, the poorest 40 percent of the population receives only one-third of the benefits from education, only one-quarter of the benefits from secondary education, and 19 percent of the benefits from tertiary education. The primary school dropout rate is two-thirds. The poorest 37 percent of the population only receives one-quarter of the benefits from health expenditure; most health expenditure is on curative, not primary, care. Social security benefits (almost 10 percent of GDP) accrue almost exclusively to the nonpoor, and, although payroll taxes are high, the system's benefit levels and eligibility are rather generous.

We can conclude that, *in principle*, public expenditure rather than taxation is a more appropriate means of improving income distribution. Thus, governments that set a goal of redistributing income through public spending can do so if they are willing to pay due attention to the details of the programs that absorb the public funds. But in reality benefits are too frequently captured by the middle classes or even by the rich. This also has important implications for fiscal policies during periods of macroeconomic and structural adjustment, which I will discuss in the next section.

Structural Reforms

In recent years, structural reforms have accompanied macroeconomic stabilization efforts in many countries to create the conditions for greater economic efficiency and sustained growth. Important distributional issues can arise during the reform period. There is a real possibility that the implementation of reform measures has negative effects on employment and income distribution. While the protection of social expenditure and the implementation of safety nets could help mitigate some of these adverse effects, there is a danger that the benefits from these programs are largely captured by the nonpoor.

Short-Term Employment Effects

Structural reforms aim to promote growth and productivity, and to the extent that these reforms succeed economic growth will create more jobs and increase labor demand. However, it may take some time before these positive effects become evident. In the short term, the effect on employment can be negative for three reasons. First, structural reform often changes the structure of labor demand from the manufacturing of nontraded to traded goods. Labor demand will decline in the shrinking sectors, especially if they were subsidized and characterized by labor hoarding. This effect will be particularly strong if labor markets are liberalized and labor shedding is facilitated. At the same time, output growth in new or expanding industries may be achieved through new high-productivity jobs with relatively small employment growth. Second, to the extent that structural reform includes privatization of public enterprises or reduction in the size of the civil service, many public sector employees will lose their jobs. In the past, public enterprises and the civil service were often used as vehicles to create employment.[2] Third, a more open economy will lead to more rapid adoption of technical change. This will force previously protected firms to become more efficient. At the beginning of the adjustment, at least, there may be a reduction in labor demand.

In summary, adjustment programs with major structural reforms may in the short run increase economic more than employment growth. Countries may even be faced with an increase in official unemployment rates. Argentina's far-reaching structural adjustment program, for example, which included tax reform, deregulation, privatization, and civil-service reform, resulted for several years in a significant increase in economic growth. But substantial employment reduction in public enterprises and the civil service was not accompanied by significant gains in aggregate employment. Before the recession of 1995, annual economic growth averaged almost 8 percent while employment growth was less than 3 percent per year, resulting in a near doubling of unemployment between 1990 and 1994 to over 12 percent. By 1995, the unemployment rate had reached 18 percent. In Peru, real growth rose to more than 5 percent per year during the reform period (1991–95) while the unemployment rate rose to 8.4 percent. In Chile, unemployment increased in the early years of adjustment and reached 12 percent in 1985. Economic growth, however, has increased labor demand significantly since then, and unemployment declined to below 5 percent in 1993. Other countries also experienced an increase in unemployment following major structural reforms.

Wealth Effects

Structural adjustment also impacts the distribution of economic assets such as human capital, shares in enterprises, agricultural and urban land, industrial structures, machinery and equipment, houses, money, foreign exchange and deposits, and old cars and other durable consumer goods.

Structural reform can reduce the value of labor skills, especially in traditional or formerly protected sectors. Rising demand for those who have desirable skills pushes up wages in modern and expanding sectors. The wages of those with traditional skills fall, leading to a less even distribution of wages. Similarly, machines and structures that become obsolete and cannot easily be put to alternative uses may lose their value. Over time, however, buildings may be converted to different uses.

Those who own stock are likely to do well in the postadjustment period. Stock markets have often posted spectacular increases, and market capitalization — for example, in Argentina — increased more than tenfold between 1990 and 1993. In Mexico, there was a more than twentyfold increase between 1987 and 1993. Land values are also likely to rise, especially for agricultural land that is used to produce export crops and urban land whose value benefits from the frequent postadjustment housing and construction booms. Depending on the concentration and distribution of landownership, this can have significant distributional effects. Some owners may find themselves becoming richer without much effort. A more open economy is likely to lead to a decline in the value of used consumer durables and cars when very high tariffs come down. High inflation or large devaluations, however, can have the opposite effect. In both cases, the effect on the poor would be small, as most of these items are possessed by the more wealthy population groups. Lower inflation and realistic exchange rates are likely to increase the value of financial assets, both those held abroad and those held locally in foreign or domestic currency. The lower inflation tax is likely to benefit the less affluent relatively more, but fewer exchange restrictions will help the nonpoor.

Furthermore, there is a group of potential "winners" from reform whose gains will be perceived as unjust: those who had access to financial or fixed assets on advantageous terms (subsidized credits or exchange rates or government favors). They may now benefit a second time from the appreciation in asset prices. In sum, adjustment programs with major structural reforms are likely to bring about major changes in the country's distribution of wealth, and some of these changes may not be in a desirable direction.

Social Safety Nets

At the beginning, I noted that it is very important to possess good information on who the poor are and how they benefit from public expenditure programs. This information is critical in integrating social safety nets in reform programs, including those supported by the IMF. The integration of targeted social safety nets into adjustment programs would help improve income distribution without negative effects on economic growth. Social safety nets could include targeted income support to the affected population groups such as certain retrenched workers in public enterprises and civil servants. While the best intentions and information can result in well-designed adjustment programs and safety nets, political pressures may also require governments to "buy" support for adjustment from the nonpoor. This could mean extending benefits to the middle classes and in the process reducing the redistributional impact of public expenditure.

Policy Implications

Many of us today look at Southeast Asia for good policy lessons, equitable growth, and relatively low public expenditure. Outside of Asia, Chile and New Zealand are the main countries that draw considerable attention in this respect. Table 5.3 shows that income distribution is much more equal in the Asian tigers than in Latin America, while public expenditure levels are much lower in the former group of countries. One of the main differences between the two country groups seems to lie in the incidence of benefits from public expenditure. Social expenditure focusing on basic health and education in Southeast Asian countries has broadened the human capital base and thereby provided a large share of the population with new economic opportunities. Fiscal conservatism helped maintain macroeconomic stability and kept wasteful rent seeking at bay (World Bank 1993a).

What policy implications can be drawn for fiscal policies that promote equity and growth?

Tax policies should be efficient, broad based, and equitable, but tax policy alone cannot achieve distributional objectives.

The benefits from social expenditure such as health, education, and basic social assistance should be targeted particularly to low-income groups.

Less productive expenditure should be reduced.

In adjustment programs, targeted, efficient, and clearly pro-poor public expenditure programs should be protected.

Only well-targeted social safety nets should be implemented during adjustment periods.

However, the widespread implementation of poorly planned or managed expenditure policies, especially in Latin America, raises a more fundamental question. Postulating good policies is not enough, and bad policies may be the result of bad institutions. The "rules of the game" may have to change to improve the policy outcome (Tanzi and Schuknecht 1995). Therefore, there is a strong need to

> Improve institutional incentive structures, introduce rules rather than discretion, strengthen transparency and accountability, and strengthen budgetary procedures.
>
> Increase private sector involvement in social services and infrastructure, especially when public sector services are inefficient.
>
> Minimize government involvement. In industrial countries, for example, public transfers are better targeted when they absorb a smaller share of GDP (table 5.4). The effect of additional redistribution on disposable income is also very small; countries with public expenditure amounting to more than 50 percent of GDP

TABLE 5.3.   Public Expenditure and Income Distribution in Latin America and Southeast Asia, c. 1960 and c. 1990

	Central Government Expenditure in Percentage of GDP		Income Share of Poorest 40 Percent of Households	
	About 1970	Early 1990s	About 1970	Early 1990s
Latin America				
Argentina	19[a]	29	14	14
Brazil	29	32	9	7
Chile	36	20	13[b]	17
Costa Rica	20	26	12	13
Honduras	—	23	7[a]	9
Mexico	13	24	10	12[c]
Average	23	26	11	12
Southeast Asia				
Hong Kong	—	16	15[b]	16
Korea	18	18	18	20
Malaysia	30	26	11	14
Singapore	20	20	—	15
Thailand	18	16	15	16
Average	22	19	15	16

Source: International Monetary Fund, *Government Finance Statistics,* various issues; World Bank 1993b, 1994.
[a] 1978.
[b] 1960s.
[c] 1980s.

TABLE 5.4. Targeting of Transfers and Change in Income Distribution in Industrial Countries

| | Share of Subsidies and Transfers (percentage of GDP) | Share of Transfers to Poorest Households | | Change in Disposable Income of Poorest 40 Percent of Households[a] |
		20 Percent	20–40 Percent	
"Big" governments[b]	30.6	22.2	21.8	2.7
"Medium-sized" governments[c]	21.5	25.2	22.5	2.2
"Small" governments[d]	14.0	33.6	22.1	2.1

Source: OECD 1995 and Zandvakili 1994.

[a] Change in income share of poorest 40 percent of households due to taxation and transfers.

[b] Governments with public expenditure exceeding 50 percent of GDP in 1990: Sweden, Belgium, the Netherlands, and Italy.

[c] Governments whose public expenditure share was between 40 and 50 percent of GDP in 1990: Canada, France, Germany, and Ireland.

[d] Governments whose share of public expenditure was less than 40 percent in 1990: Australia, the United Kingdom, the United States, and Switzerland.

spend over 30 percent of GDP on subsidies and transfers, over 15 percent more than small governments with public expenditure below 40 percent GDP. However, the income share of the poorest 40 percent of households improves only by 2.7 percent in countries with big governments compared to 2.1 for countries with small governments.

NOTES

This essay was originally presented at the conference Economic Growth and Equity: International Experience and Policies, July 12–13, 1996, Santiago, Chile. Assistance received from Ludger Schuknecht is greatly appreciated. The views expressed are strictly those of the author and not necessarily those of the IMF.

1. The study looks at Gini coefficients in 88 developing and developed countries during the period 1960–95.

2. Public sector retrenchment often affects members of the middle classes, who hold most civil service and public enterprise posts. However, one civil service salary often supports a large number of family members, and the loss of this income could push them into poverty.

REFERENCES

Deininger, Klaus, and Lyn Squire. 1995. "Inequality and Growth: Results from a New Data Set." World Bank. Mimeo.

International Monetary Fund. *Government Finance Statistics* (Washington, DC). Various issues.

Organization for Economic Cooperation and Development. 1995. "Income Distribution in OECD Countries." *Social Policy Studies,* no. 18. Paris: OECD.

Petrei, A. Humberto. 1987. *El Gasto Público Social y sus Efectos Distributivos: Un Examen Comparativo de Cinco países de América Latina.* Rio de Janeiro: Programa ECIEL.

———. 1995. "Distribución Del Ingreso: El Papel Del Gasto Público Social." Paper presented at the seventh Seminar of Fiscal Policy, Santiago, Chile.

Schwartz, Gerd, and Teresa Ter-Minassian. 1995. "The Distributional Effects of Public Expenditure: Update and Overview." IMF Working Paper WP/95/84. Washington, DC, International Monetary Fund.

Tanzi, Vito. 1974. "Redistributing Income through the Budget in Latin America." *Banca Nazionale Del Lavoro Quarterly Review* 108 (1974):65–87.

———. 1995. "Macroeconomic Adjustment with Major Structural Reforms: Implications for Employment and Income Distribution." Paper presented at the IMF conference Income Distribution and Sustainable Growth, April 1995, Washington, DC.

Tanzi, Vito, and Ludger Schuknecht. 1995. "The Growth of Government and the Reform of the State in Industrial Countries." IMF Working Paper WP/95/130. Washington, DC, International Monetary Fund.

World Bank. 1993a. *The East Asian Miracle.* Washington, DC: World Bank.

———. 1993b. *Social Indicators of Development.* Washington, DC: World Bank.

———. 1994. *Social Indicators of Development.* Washington, DC: World Bank.

Zandvakili, S. 1994. "Redistribution through Taxation: An International Comparison." *Empirical Economics,* 473–91.

CHAPTER 6

Growth and Inequality: Do Regional Patterns Redeem Kuznets?

Barbara Stallings, Nancy Birdsall, and Julie Clugage

The topic of income distribution and its relation to economic growth has been put back on the international agenda by the performance of the East Asian economies, where results defied conventional wisdom over a significant period of time. In that part of the world, positive rates of growth were combined with high levels of income equality over more than three decades, a record well worth close analysis (World Bank 1993) despite the recent problems in the region. This record contrasts with the pessimism underlying the well-known analysis of Simon Kuznets, who suggested that distribution would worsen during early periods of rapid growth, and Nicholas Kaldor, who argued for the need for an unequal distribution of income to encourage growth because of the higher savings propensity among the wealthy.

The East Asian results are of particular interest to regions of the developing world that are trying to restore growth rates after repeated bouts of crisis and recession (Latin America and Africa), to emerge from sharp economic decline following major restructuring of their economic systems (Eastern Europe and the former Soviet republics), or to speed up traditionally slow growth rates (South Asia). All would like to be able to do so without having to suffer increases in inequality. This concern is especially acute in Latin America, where distribution of income is the most unequal in the world.

This essay aims to make a contribution to the revived debate by focusing on differences across regions in the nature of the relationship between growth and distribution, with special emphasis on the mechanisms behind these different relationships. In this sense, it complements recent studies that use cross-country analysis to model the relationship between growth and distribution either by regressing income on distribution or vice versa (à la Kuznets).[1] These studies, which we summarize in the first section, have not taken advantage of differences across regions in the relationship between growth and income inequality to explore the mechanisms behind those differences. We do so here by comparing the relationship across regions between average growth and average equality over the period 1965–92.[2] Next, we present a closer comparison of the East Asian and Latin American cases, arguing that the contrast between them in the intraregional relationship of average growth and average inequality can be explained by the nature of the urbanization and industrialization process emphasized by Kuznets. Specifically, we argue that the economic patterns he hypothesized to support his "inverted U" relationship between income and inequality (and other economic patterns consistent with his hypothesis) are at the heart of a "virtuous circle" in East Asia and a "vicious circle" in Latin America.[3] We conclude with some remarks on the possible policy implications of our analysis.

Recent Analyses of the Growth-Inequality Relationship

The growth-inequality relationship — across countries and over time within countries — has been the focus of much of the recent growth literature. Due to the absence of quality time-series data for individual countries, most empirical studies exploring the Kuznets hypothesis have used cross-country data to test the relationship. Through the 1970s, studies seemed to validate the initial tradeoff between growth and equality observed by Kuznets (e.g., Ahluwalia 1976). In fact, Robinson (1976) observed that the hypothesis about an inevitable tradeoff between growth and equality had "acquired the force of economic law."

More recent studies, however, have demonstrated that empirical tests of the inverted-U relationship between growth and inequality are highly sensitive to changes in functional form and to the choice of observations (Anand and Kanbur 1993). Using higher quality income distribution data for a cross-section of countries, many analysts have failed to find a worldwide, statistically significant, inverted-U relationship (Bruno, Ravallion, and Squire in this volume; Anand and Kanbur 1993; Fishlow 1996; Deininger and Squire 1996c; Schultz 1997).

Most studies of the impact of inequality on growth (rather than vice versa) have found a significantly negative impact of initial income inequality on subsequent growth. East Asia has served as a stimulus for this work, as have East Asia–Latin America comparisons. Virtually all of the analysis has been based on reduced-form equations, with the explanatory variables including one or more measures of income inequality. For example, Rodrik (1994), using initial per capita GDP, initial primary and secondary school enrollment, the investment/GDP ratio, and population growth, is able to "explain" 46 percent of the variance of per capita GDP growth for 1960–85. By adding Gini coefficients for the distribution of income and land at the beginning of the period, he increases his R^2 from .46 to .67.

Even these results, however, have not gone without question. Fishlow (1996), using a different sample of countries and inequality data from a later period, finds no significant impact of initial inequality on growth. He attributes his different findings in part to the poor quality of income inequality observations prior to the 1960s and to the fact that he includes a dummy variable for Latin America. Deininger and Squire (1996c) go further: using a newly created set of high-quality income distribution data,[4] they challenge the existence of any systematic, worldwide relationship between distribution and growth.[5]

Several of the studies that do find a significant impact of initial inequality on subsequent growth argue that the effect is channeled through political instability. While Rodrik argues that political stability is one of the reasons for the importance of equality, other studies have specifically included political factors as explanatory variables (Sachs 1989; Larrain and Vergara 1992; Alesina and Rodrik 1994; Persson and Tabellini 1994). Persson and Tabellini explain per capita growth between 1960 and 1985 as a function of the following independent variables: initial income distribution, initial GDP, initial primary school attendance, and political participation (measured by a dummy for democracies). Inclusion of the political variables raised the R^2 from .32 to .44. Splitting the sample into democracies and nondemocracies, the distributional variable was significant only for the former subgroup.[6]

Persson and Tabellini make the general statement on the link between political factors and the growth-equality relationship that "income inequality is harmful for growth, because it leads to policies that do not protect property rights and do not allow full private appropriation of returns from investment" (1994, 617). Other authors are more specific. For example, Alesina and Rodrik (1994) hypothesize that high inequality in a democracy is likely to be associated with high taxes, which discourage investment and lead to low growth. Larrain and Vergara (1992) suggest that high inequality leads directly to instability, which discourages investment. Sachs (1989) argues that high inequality leads to frequent changes in governments, instability of policies, populism, and low investment. Li, Squire, and Zou (1996), in contrast to the majority-rule models in other analyses, assume that the richest group in a society can influence economic policy through its economic power or direct political control rather than through a voting mechanism. The rich do so in a way that protects their own interests, creating what amounts to a tax on the rest of the society.[7] Insofar as inequality does limit growth, this political mechanism has a negative economic impact.

Cross-Regional Patterns of Growth
and Income Inequality

In addition to Fishlow 1996, many other studies of the growth-equality relationship (e.g., Schultz 1997) find significant regional dummy variables, implying that there are unique regional patterns worth exploring. This is precisely what we do here. We do not challenge analyses, such as the one in chapter 3 of this volume, that reject an overall relationship; rather, we want to examine the intraregional and cross-regional differences in the growth-distribution relationship. First, using Deininger and Squire's (1996a) new data for income distribution across countries, together with the Penn World Tables (Summers and Heston 1995) for growth, we present a snapshot of the relationship in many countries between average growth and average equality over the period 1965–92 (fig. 6.1). We note a marked tendency for countries of a particular region to cluster in terms of the equality measure (in this case, the ratio of the income share of the top 20 percent of the population to the bottom 20 percent). Table 6.1 shows for each region the average and the range for that measure, together with per capita income and poverty incidence. The mostly likely explanation for the clustering phenomenon is that region is acting as a proxy for the level of development (per capita income) and, as we will suggest, for "style" of development as well.

There are two regions with relatively low inequality, where the richest quintile has less than 10 times the income of the poorest quintile. One is Europe, which includes many of the richest countries in the world, where the top 20 percent has between four and nine times the income share of the bottom 20 percent, with an average of 5.5. With the exception of Canada, other industrial countries are somewhat more unequal. For Japan, the most recent income distribution data indicate that the top 20 percent has 7.1 times the income of the bottom quintile; the ratio is 9.8 in the United States and 10.1 in Australia.

The other low-inequality region is South Asia. These countries, among the poorest in the world, have an average distribution ratio of 5.4, very similar to that of Europe and lower than that of some other industrial nations. The relative equality in the two regions is what a cross-sectional version of the Kuznets hypothesis would predict: the richest and poorest nations have the lowest inequality.

A third region also fits the cross-sectional Kuznets pattern: Latin America, a middle-income region, has the highest degree of inequality. As shown in table 6.1 and figure 6.1, the richest 20 percent of the population in Latin American countries has captured, on average over the period 1965–92, about 16 times the income of the poorest. These data provide support for the statement that the Latin American region is

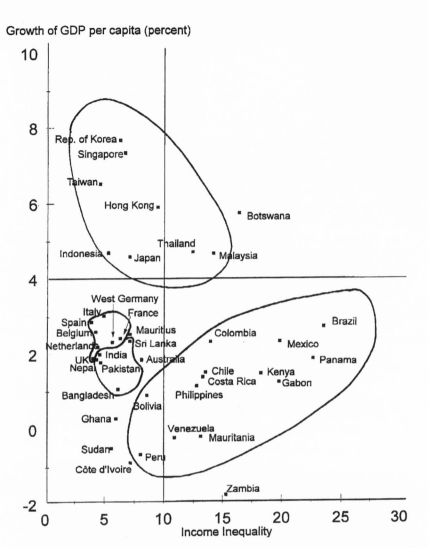

Fig. 6.1. Income inequality and growth of GDP, 1965–92. (Data from Deininger and Squire 1996a for income inequality; and Penn World Tables [Summers and Heston 1995] for growth.) *Note:* Income inequality is measured as the ratio of the income share of the richest 20 percent to the share of the poorest 20 percent of the population. Observation is the average of high-quality data available for 1965–92. Growth data are unavailable for the Sudan (1970–91), Taiwan (1965–90), and Zambia (1965–91).

the most unequal in the world. If additional Latin American nations were included, the ratio would increase.

A fourth region, East Asia, also shows marked clustering among countries, though not in the Kuznets pattern. This is a region of middle-income countries where inequality is low. On average, the top quintile receives 7.9 times the income of the bottom quintile; this ratio is higher than that of European countries and South Asia but much lower than that of Latin America and sub-Saharan Africa. This group of Asian nations not only deviates from the Kuznets predictions on a cross-sectional basis but also dynamically. As will be discussed, these countries have increased their per capita income very rapidly, and most seem to have improved their distributional profile in the process.[8]

One region presents an exception to clustering: sub-Saharan Africa, where data problems are the most serious. Probably for this reason, in addition to the great variety of situations on the continent, income distribution measures for sub-Saharan African countries vary enormously. The average figure for the countries with data available is 13.1, similar to Latin America but with a much higher variance.

Turning to the (static) growth-equality relationship within each region, we can observe three different patterns in figure 6.1. First, there are three regions with no systematic relationship between growth and equality. These include both the richest countries (Europe and, more

TABLE 6.1.   Per Capita Income, Distribution, and Poverty

Region[a]	Per Capita Income (1991 U.S.$)[b]		Income Distribution[c]		Poverty (1980–90)[b,d] (% of population)
	Nominal	PPP[e]	Average	Range	
OECD	$19,048	$16,245	6.47	3.9/15.2	na
Europe[f]	$18,344	$15,809	5.54	3.9/8.9	na
Asia					
East Asia and the Pacific	$3,071[g]	$5,163[g]	7.88	4.2/14.2	39[g]
South Asia	$327	$1,447	5.36	4.3/7.1	54
Latin America and the Caribbean	$2,473	$4,455	16.24	8.6/27.7	44
Sub-Saharan Africa	$540	$1,250	13.1	4.0/28.6	54

[a]Regional groupings are according to World Bank 1996.

[b]Data from United Nations Development Program 1994.

[c]Richest 20%/poorest 20%. Data from Deininger and Squire 1996a. Each observation is the average of all high-quality data available for the period 1965–92.

[d]Rural data were used when no national data were available.

[e]Purchasing power parity.

[f]An OECD subgroup including the 12 members of the European Union as of 1992.

[g]Data not available for Taiwan.

broadly, the industrial world) and the poorest countries (South Asia and sub-Saharan Africa). Within each of these three regions, the dispersion of data points suggests that growth patterns are substantially independent of equality.

A second pattern — that of a negative relationship between average growth and equality — is evident within Latin America. In the Latin America group, the highest growth over the 27-year period is in precisely those countries with the lowest levels of equality.

Finally, within East Asia, the relationship between average growth and equality appears to be positive. The four East Asian nations (Korea, Taiwan, Hong Kong, and Singapore) have both the highest growth and the greatest equality, while their four Southeast Asian neighbors have somewhat poorer records on both. This combination produces the positive correlation. The Philippines has the worst record, with both lesser equality and lower growth performance. (Indeed, it was once common among Asian experts to refer to the Philippines as a "quasi–Latin American country." The graph illustrates one of the reasons for this label since the Philippines falls within the Latin American rather than the Asian cluster.)

In summary, cross-regional comparisons generally tend to reveal regional clusters with respect to the growth-equality relationship. Also, there seem to be distinct intraregional patterns in the relationship between average growth and average equality. While there is considerable controversy over the nature of the link (if any) between growth and equality for the world as a whole, a clear relationship does emerge between the two variables within two regions — Latin America and East Asia — and the patterns take, interestingly, opposite forms.

Latin America and East Asia

Indeed, Latin America and East Asia provide crucial cases for examining the growth-equality relationship in more detail. Table 6.2 summarizes the differences for seven countries in each region.[9] On the equality variable, Asia's performance is generally far better than that of Latin America. Only Thailand approaches Latin American levels of inequality, and its ratio is less than the Latin American average. As the first two columns show, the cross-regional difference arises both from a higher income share for the bottom 20 percent and a lower share for the upper 20 percent in East Asia. With respect to growth, there is no overlap at all: all Asian countries grew faster than their Latin American counterparts in the 27-year period.

Figure 6.2 shows the situation for the two regions during the

1980s, when the contrast was greatest. This was the "lost decade" for Latin America but a period of great dynamism in Asia. The two patterns are clear: Latin America clusters with low growth and low equality, while Asia displays the opposite characteristics. The exception is again the Philippines, which is located squarely within the Latin American cluster because of its low growth performance — although it is more equal than any Latin American country.

When taken as a single group of countries (as in fig. 6.2), East Asia and Latin America appear to provide strong evidence for a positive cross-sectional relationship between average growth and average equality. The same is true for East Asia alone but not for Latin America. What, then, are the mechanisms that distinguish the two?

Most of the empirical studies mentioned previously rely heavily on political factors to explain the positive relationship between initial equality and subsequent growth. The median voter theory explains the tendency toward populism and poor fiscal policies in Latin America. The benefits of political stability explain what were high levels of private investment in East Asia. However, the regional patterns we have

TABLE 6.2.   Income Distribution and Growth: Latin America and Asia

Country	Poorest 20% of Population (% of national income)	Richest 20% of Population (% of national income)	Ratio (2/1)	Average Annual per Capita GDP Growth, 1965–92 (%)
Asia				
Hong Kong	4.9	49.4	10.1	5.9
Indonesia	8.7	40.7	4.7	4.7
Korea, Rep.	7.4	42.2	5.7	7.7 (65–91)
Malaysia	4.6	53.7	11.7	4.7
Singapore	6.5	46.6	7.2	7.4
Taiwan	7.1	38.7	5.4	6.5 (65–90)
Thailand	3.7	58.5	15.8	4.7
Philippines	5.2	52.5	10.1	1.1
Average	6.0	47.8	8.8	5.3
Latin America				
Argentina	n/a	n/a	n/a	−0.3 (65–90)
Brazil	2.5	65.2	26.3	2.7
Chile	3.5	61.0	17.3	1.5
Colombia	3.6	54.4	15.1	2.3
Mexico	3.2	59.3	18.5	2.3
Peru	4.9	50.4	10.3	−0.7
Venezuela	3.6	58.4	16.2	−0.2
Average	3.6	58.1	17.3	1.1

Note: Income share data are the latest high-quality observations available from Deininger and Squire 1996a. Growth data are from the Penn World Tables (Summers and Heston 1995).

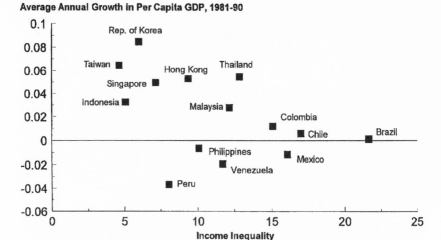

Fig. 6.2. Income inequality and GDP per capita growth rate, 1981–90. (Data from Deininger and Squire 1996a for income inequality; and Penn World Tables [Summers and Heston 1995] for growth.) *Note:* Income inequality is measured as the ratio of the income share of the richest 20 percent of the population to the share of the poorest 20 percent. Observations are an average of the high-quality data available over the period 1981–90.

emphasized, and particularly the opposite patterns we note for East Asia and Latin America, can also be explained by more fundamental differences in economic structure and policies (which admittedly have affected politics). Kuznets, indeed, may have had the economics of the story right (i.e., the urbanization and industrialization process may involve increases in inequality in the absence of corrective policies), even though empirical outcomes across regions and countries and within countries over time follow no neat pattern. The Kuznets argument (1955) suggests that a temporary negative link between growth and equality results from the shift from low-income and low-inequality agriculture to high-income and high-inequality industry, which creates an income gap between the two sectors and more inequality overall with more workers in the higher inequality sector. If the industry is capital intensive, the gap is exacerbated, and if government policy favors capital-intensive industry the situation is even more extreme. Though Kuznets did not focus on human capital, a second reason for a temporary negative link could be a low education stock, such that the demand for skilled workers exceeds the supply, creating within the industrial sector an additional gap between the wages of skilled versus unskilled labor.

All of these explanations are based on the transition from a relatively homogeneous work force to one that is more heterogeneous (and then eventually to a new work force at the higher levels of income). The processes described Latin America's pattern of development much better than that of East Asia, where the relation between average growth and average equality since the 1960s has been negative, as Kuznets suggested. For example, the productivity differential between agriculture and industry was probably higher in Latin America than in Asia because of the explicit decision in Latin America to promote industry at the expense of agriculture and because of the historically unequal distribution of land in the region.[10] These factors mean that migration out of agriculture had a more negative impact on distribution in Latin America than in other regions. Likewise, the secondary (although not the primary) education stock was lower in Latin America than in East Asia in the early 1960s, meaning that there was a larger wage premium in Latin America for those completing secondary education and a larger wage gap between skilled and unskilled workers.[11] In sum, Latin America had a much more diverse work force (in terms of access to assets) than did East Asia as it embarked upon its economic transition, and the differences among workers were exacerbated during the process of industrialization. It is not surprising, then, that a negative relationship between average growth and average equality has existed within Latin America, nor that Latin America fits well into a cross-sectional analysis of the Kuznets hypothesis.

There is even some evidence of a dynamic inverted-U relationship between growth and inequality within certain Latin American countries. It is striking that three of the five countries worldwide where Deininger and Squire (1996c) do find an inverted-U relationship fall within Latin America (the fourth is the Philippines). Londoño (1995) also finds an inverted-U path for inequality over time in Colombia by using data going back to the 1930s.

Some recent empirical studies focus on economic characteristics and economic policies to explain why, in effect, the stylized facts associated with Kuznets have not applied to East Asia. For example, in the World Bank's "East Asian Miracle" study (World Bank 1993) the importance is stressed of policies that link growth and equality by rapidly eliminating the initial productivity differences between agriculture and industry emphasized by Kuznets (Kuo, Ranis, and Fei 1981). The postwar land reform programs in Korea, Taiwan, and Japan contributed to the elimination of these productivity differences by equalizing access to resources across households.[12] Also, policies that promoted human capital and provided incentives for labor-intensive exports rapidly reduced the scarcity rents to physical and human capital that create inequality. According to the World Bank analysis, these variables, together with policies that supported macroeconomic stability in East Asia, were the main factors distinguishing the "high-performing Asian economies" from others, especially their Latin American counterparts. In East Asia, these policies involved the poor in the growth process and minimized any increase in work force heterogeneity, and the associated inequality, during the industrialization process.

Birdsall and her colleagues (e.g., Birdsall, Ross, and Sabot 1995) have placed special emphasis on how a high demand for labor accelerates the reduction of differentials in productivity and wages. They note that differences among countries in the demand for labor have been neglected in regression studies of growth that test the contribution of education; the resulting omitted-variable in these regressions may be a factor in the substantial overprediction of rates of growth for some countries with higher than predicted rates of enrollment in primary and secondary schools in the 1960s but low demand for labor. For example, a country such as Argentina, like the East Asian economies, had a greater human capital endowment than was predicted for its initial levels of income. Weak demand for labor, including educated labor, may help explain why it nevertheless tended to underperform with respect to growth. A similar situation occurred in countries like Egypt, the Philippines, Sri Lanka, and the former Soviet Union. In contrast, high levels of demand for workers in East Asia, initially for unskilled but eventually for skilled workers, drove average wages up.

It is widely acknowledged that macroeconomic, agricultural, and, in particular, export-push policies contributed to a high demand for labor in East Asia (World Bank 1993). Did these policies, by ensuring adequate demand for skilled as well as unskilled labor, also help ensure a high economic return to education in East Asia, accelerating its accumulation even more? Birdsall, Ross, and Sabot (1995) report results of a regression in which the supply of education is controlled and the relevance of the demand for skills is tested (using variables that measure the degree to which an economy is oriented toward manufactured exports). Although weak, the results are consistent with the view that the stimulus provided by the greater supply of human capital for economic growth will be augmented where there is high demand for labor—particularly skilled labor—as in East Asia, where the export orientation of economies resulted in a skill-demanding growth path. This finding is also consistent with the shift of East Asian exporters into more technologically sophisticated and capital- and skill-intensive goods, as rapidly ris-

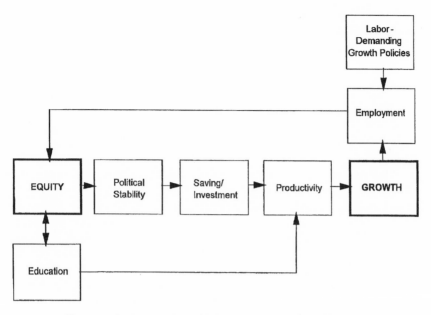

Fig. 6.3.   Positive relationships between growth and equity.

ing wages of unskilled labor eroded international competitiveness in labor-intensive manufactured goods. Thus, the combination of a greater supply of education and a greater demand for educated workers contributed to faster economic growth in East Asia than in other developing regions, including Latin America.

One way to summarize the previous discussion is to think in terms of virtuous versus vicious circles. Two economic variables are critical to the process: education and an outward-looking economic policy, which, via exports and/or the adoption of new labor-intensive technologies, generate a labor-demanding growth path. Figure 6.3 shows that education makes a positive contribution to equality (which increases political stability), leading to high savings and investment. The high investment, in turn, increases productivity,[13] which is also raised by education. Higher productivity leads to higher growth, which increases employment, especially in outward-oriented economies in which labor-intensive technology is stressed, and feeds back to increase equality. This is the virtuous circle found in East Asia. The vicious circle, which has been more common in Latin America, features just the opposite characteristics: low education has reinforced high inequality and low productivity growth, high political instability, low savings, and low investment. Low savings and investment have slowed productivity and output growth. Until the reforms of the last decade, inward-looking policies, together with emphasis on capital-intensive industry, led to low employment generation and continuing (or even exacerbated) inequality.

Policy Implications

What are the policy implications of this analysis? Given Asia's impressive performance over several decades with respect to growth and equality (the stated goal of most Latin American governments), why have more lessons not been drawn and implemented? What, if anything, can Latin America learn from Asia?

Looking at these issues from the perspective of 1998, in the midst of the financial crisis that has wreaked havoc on many of the East Asian nations, some might question whether East Asia has any lessons to offer. This would be a serious error. While the ongoing crisis clearly raises a number of questions, including some about the relationships among growth, equality, and globalization, the fact remains that these countries have managed to sustain high growth for three decades while maintaining and even decreasing income inequality.[14] Certain characteristics and policies do seem to have been associated with this notably non-Kuznetian outcome.

With respect to why more lessons have not been learned, we present a number of possibilities.

1. There may be problems of information. Before the 1980s, there was a lack of information about what was happening in Asia. Now that is no longer true. On the contrary, there may be too much information in the sense of multiple interpretations of the East Asian experience.
2. The 1980s made the East Asian experience both more relevant and more difficult to replicate in Latin America (even where there is agreement on the lessons). During the 1980s, inequality increased in Latin America (Londoño 1996) and there was a decline in social spending, so human capital formation was generally lower in the early 1990s than before the "lost decade." There were substantial capital exports from Latin America during the 1980s and thus a decline in physical capital formation. Finally, in part because of the historic bias against labor, the existing structure of production has meant that, in the reform years of the early 1990s, increased productivity could be most rapidly achieved by reducing the use of labor, leading to higher unemployment and serious

social unrest in some countries and compounding the problems of policymakers.

3. Leaving aside the new problems resulting from the 1980s, the initial conditions for East Asia in the 1960s were more favorable than for Latin America now. On the domestic front, wages were lower, so export-led growth was more viable. Internationally, markets were more open, so products could be sold, and rules were less rigid, so incentives could be given that are no longer possible.

4. Resource endowments in Northeast Asia were propitious to the development of labor-intensive and human-resource-based production. That is, ironically, the lack of natural resources turned out to be an advantage in comparison with Latin America, where a (physical) capital-intensive economic strategy allowed neglect of the development of human capital. (The resource endowment in Southeast Asia, by contrast, is similar to that of Latin America.)

5. Initial asset distribution was more equitable in East Asia than in Latin America. Important agrarian reforms had been imposed in Japan, Korea, and Taiwan, while only in a few cases had such reforms occurred in Latin America. Human capital, though not much greater on average in the 1960s, was more evenly distributed in East Asia; subsequent accumulation of human capital in the 1970s and 1980s was much greater and much more equitably distributed (Birdsall and Londoño 1997).[15]

Given this background, what can Latin America learn from East Asia? First, relevant lessons are more likely to come from Southeast rather than Northeast Asia, since there is a greater similarity of structural conditions (resource endowments and distribution of assets) with Southeast Asia. Also, the timing is more comparable: policy lessons for Latin America in the late 1990s are likely to be found in policy decisions taken in the late 1970s and 1980s in Southeast Asia rather than in the 1960s when Northeast Asia made its initial advances.[16] This suggests that the key for Latin America is not the well-known industrial policies of Northeast Asia but the export orientation and openness to foreign direct investment of Southeast Asia.

The second lesson is now widely accepted in Latin America: the need to invest in both quantitative and qualitative improvements in human capital. The problem goes beyond finding the resources: public expenditures on education in most countries of the region have been rising and by international standards are not low as a percentage of GDP. The East Asian experience indicates that attention must be paid to broad-based access to basic education of good quality; public expenditures are best directed at the primary and secondary levels unless and until most students are completing secondary school.

Third, the demand for labor, as well as its supply at each skill level, matters. The economic reforms of the last decade in most countries of Latin America,[17] which are reducing protection and emphasizing export-led growth, are designed to encourage job creation and thus to enhance both equality and growth. That this positive result has not yet occurred in most countries is arguably due to the overstaffing that accompanied the previous economic model in Latin America.

Fourth, given the increasing evidence of a close link between growth and the distribution of assets, a critical lesson for Latin America is the importance of ensuring that the poor have access not only to education but to credit, property rights, and, in general, equal economic opportunities. Redistribution of assets is one means of increasing the assets of the poor. Redistribution of land has been limited and politically difficult, although Brazil and Colombia, among other countries, are now initiating market-based reform programs that hold promise. It is impossible, of course, to redistribute the existing stock of education, but emphasis on the creation of new assets[18] via larger public investments in education makes sense. If this is to be a solution, the distribution of these new assets will be crucial (e.g., while educational reform cannot affect the stock of human capital, it must ensure a better distribution of the flow).

Finally, policies beyond redistribution and human capital formation have the potential to promote both faster growth and greater equality simultaneously. Based on the Asian experience, Birdsall, Pinckney, and Sabot (1996) suggest policies that are likely to increase the savings of the poor (and thus their access to assets). ECLAC has put forward a series of proposals for achieving growth with equity (ECLAC 1990, 1992; Ramos 1995); a crucial one is to ensure that small and medium-sized enterprises, the major source of employment, have access to capital, technology, and management know-how, through government programs if necessary.[19] The development of infrastructure is another area with the potential to increase both growth and income equality since it clearly increases productivity and provides employment.

The experiences of one region, with its own historical, cultural, and political characteristics, cannot be directly imported by another. But East Asia's performance over three decades holds lessons for Latin America despite the recent difficulties. The education-cum-labor absorption nexus so central to East Asia's success can be adapted to the Latin American context. Adaptation will be more politically difficult because of Latin America's high income inequality, and the benefits will not come quickly, but they are likely to be substantial and sustainable if implemented in the proper policy context.

NOTES

1. Birdsall, Ross, and Sabot (1995, 1997) draw inferences about regional differences on the basis of cross-country analysis comparing East Asia and Latin America, but they do not discuss explicitly the difference in the apparent growth-distribution relationship between the two regions. See also Stallings 1995, which focuses on regions from a broader perspective.
2. We do not attempt to model the dynamic relationship Kuznets had in mind between income and inequality, within either a country or a region. This is due to a lack of high-quality time-series data and because many studies have failed to find a significant intracountry and/or intraregional relationship over time (see, e.g., Deininger and Squire 1996c and Schultz 1997). That is, we seek not to defend the famous "inverted-U" relationship Kuznets hypothesized over time for a single country but to focus on the relevance of his "stylized facts" (1955) in explaining the relationship between average growth and average inequality in different regions of the world.
3. Birdsall and Sabot (1994) use the term *virtuous circle* to describe a large number of interacting positive effects over three decades in East Asia among variables such as growth, equity, education, fertility, labor-demanding economic structure, and export orientation.
4. The three criteria that the data must meet in order to be included in the new sample are as follows: (1) they should be based on nationally representative surveys, (2) they should cover the entire population, and (3) they should encompass all important types of income. The number of resulting "high-quality" observations in the Deininger-Squire data bank is 682, compared to a maximum of 73 in the most commonly used sources (Fields 1989; Jain 1975; Paukert 1973).
5. Although they argue against an overall relationship between growth and *income* distribution, they do find a significant link between growth and the distribution of *assets* (proxied by land distribution). Birdsall and Londoño (1997) find that the initial distribution of human capital, in addition to land distribution, affects subsequent growth and that worsening inequality negatively affects the incomes of the poor.
6. It should be noted that this study is one of those criticized by Deininger and Squire (1996c). Indeed, using their new "high-quality" data, they come to the conclusion that only for nondemocracies is the equality variable significant.
7. Birdsall and James (1993) also make this point.
8. On the apparent improvements over time, see data provided in Birdsall, Ross, and Sabot 1995 (fig. 1, 480), World Bank 1993 (fig. 3), and Deininger and Squire 1996a.
9. Table 6.2 uses the most recent high-quality data on income distribution (in contrast to fig. 6.1, which uses the average over the period 1965–92).
10. See Schiff and Valdes 1992 and Engerman and Sokoloff 1994.

11. Birdsall, Ross, and Sabot (1995) document this difference for Brazil compared to Korea.

12. There also appears to be a tendency for lower inequality in Latin American countries that have enacted land reform. For example, Mexico has lower inequality than Brazil, with which it is frequently compared on other variables. Likewise, Bolivia and Peru have distributions that are more equal than in most of their regional neighbors. Chile, where the agrarian reform was reversed during the military government, saw its income distribution become more unequal during this period—although, of course, there were many other reasons for this trend.

13. Of course, there are limits even to this relationship. Recent experience suggests that some investment in East Asia was driven by and reinforced asset booms, with questionable productivity results.

14. Beginning in about 1994, it appears that high capital inflows exacerbated what was already growing asset or wealth inequality in low income–inequality countries like Korea.

15. This point needs to be considered in conjunction with the recent work suggesting that asset distribution is more important than income distribution for growth prospects.

16. The closer link between Latin America and Southeast Asia is the result of the lost decade in Latin America, since in the 1970s the large Latin American countries were frequently compared to Korea and Taiwan.

17. See Inter-American Development Bank 1996, 1997.

18. See, for example, Deininger and Squire 1996c.

19. The Asian experience is one of subcontractual links between large and small firms that spread financial, technological, and management expertise.

REFERENCES

Ahluwalia, Montek S. 1976. "Inequality, Poverty, and Development." *Journal of Development Economics* 3:307–42.

Alesina, Alberto, and Dani Rodrik. 1994. "Distributive Politics and Economic Growth." *Quarterly Journal of Economics* 108:465–90.

Anand, Sudhir, and S. M. R. Kanbur. 1993. "Inequality and Development: A Critique." *Journal of Development Economics* 40:25–52.

Birdsall, Nancy, and Estelle James. 1993. "Efficiency and Equity in Social Spending: How and Why Governments Misbehave." In Michael Lipton and Jacques Van der Gaag, eds., *Including the Poor.* Washington, DC: World Bank.

Birdsall, Nancy, and Juan Luis Londoño. 1997. "Asset Inequality Matters: An Assessment of the World Bank's Approach to Poverty Reduction." *American Economic Review* (May):32–37.

Birdsall, Nancy, Thomas Pinckney, and Richard Sabot. 1996. "Why Low Inequality Spurs Growth: Savings and Investment by the Poor." IDB OCE Working Paper. Washington, DC.

Birdsall, Nancy, David Ross, and Richard Sabot. 1995. "Inequality and Growth Reconsidered: Lessons from East Asia." *World Bank Economic Review* 9(3):477–508.

———. 1997. "Education, Growth, and Inequality." In Nancy Birdsall and Frederick Jaspersen, eds., *Pathways to Growth*. Washington, DC: Inter-American Development Bank.

Birdsall, Nancy, and Richard Sabot. 1994. "Virtuous Circles." Manuscript.

———, eds. 1996. *Opportunity Foregone: Education in Brazil*. Washington, DC: Inter-American Development Bank.

Deininger, Klaus, and Lyn Squire. 1996a. "A New Data Set Measuring Income Inequality." *World Bank Economic Review* 10(3):565–91.

———. 1996b. "Does Inequality Matter? Re-examining the Links between Growth and Equality." World Bank. Mimeo.

———. 1996c. "New Ways of Looking at Old Issues: Inequality and Growth." World Bank. Mimeo.

ECLAC (UN Economic Commission for Latin America). 1990. *Changing Production Patterns with Social Equity*. Santiago: United Nations.

———. 1992. *Social Equity and Changing Production Patterns: An Integrated Approach*. Santiago: United Nations.

Engerman, Stanley L., and Kenneth L. Sokoloff. 1994. "Factor Endowments, Institutions, and Differential Paths of Growth among New World Economies: A View from Economic Historians of the United States." NBER Working Paper H0066, National Bureau of Economic Research, Cambridge, MA.

Fields, Gary S. 1989. "A Compendium of Data on Inequality and Poverty for the Developing World." Cornell University, Department of Economics. Mimeo.

Fishlow, Albert. 1996. "Inequality, Poverty, and Growth: Where Do We Stand?" In Michael Bruno and Boris Pleskovic, eds., *Annual World Bank Conference on Development Economics, 1995*, 25–39. Washington, DC: World Bank.

Inter-American Development Bank. 1996. *Economic and Social Progress in Latin America*. Washington, DC: Inter-American Development Bank.

———. 1997. *Economic and Social Progress in Latin America*. Washington, DC: Inter-American Development Bank.

Jain, Shail. 1975. *Size Distribution of Income: A Compilation of Data*. Washington, DC: World Bank.

Kuo, Shirley W. Y., Gustav Ranis, and John C. H. Fei. 1981. *The Taiwan Success Story: Rapid Growth with Improved Distribution in the Republic of China, 1952–1979*. Boulder: Westview Press.

Kuznets, Simon. 1955. "Economic Growth and Income Inequality." *American Economic Review* 45:1–28.

Larraín, Felipe, and Rodrigo Vergara. 1992. "Distribución del ingreso, inversión y crecimiento." *Cuadernos de Economía*, no. 87:207–28.

Li, Hongyi, Lyn Squire, and Heng-fu Zou. 1996. "Explaining International and Intertemporal Variations in Income Inequality." World Bank, Policy Research Department. Mimeo.

Londoño, Juan Luis. 1995. *Distribución del ingreso y desarrollo económico: Colombia en el siglo XX.* Bogota: Tercer Mundo.

————. 1996. *Poverty, Inequality, and Human Capital Development in Latin America, 1950–2025.* World Bank Latin American and Caribbean Studies, Viewpoints. Washington, DC: World Bank.

Paukert, Felix. 1973. "Income Distribution at Different Levels of Development: A Survey of Evidence." *International Labour Review* 108, nos. 2–3:97–125.

Persson, Torsten, and Guido Tabellini. 1994. "Is Inequality Harmful to Growth?" *American Economic Review* 84:600–21.

Ramos, Joseph. 1995. "Can Growth and Equity Go Hand in Hand?" *CEPAL Review* 56:13–24.

Robinson, Sherman. 1976. "A Note on the U-Hypothesis Relating Income Inequality and Economic Development." *American Economic Review* 66, no. 3:437–40.

Rodrik, Dani. 1994. "King Kong Meets Godzilla: The World Bank and the East Asian Miracle." In Albert Fishlow et al., eds., *Miracle or Design? Lessons from the East Asian Experience.* Washington, DC: Overseas Development Council.

Sachs, Jeffrey. 1989. "Social Conflict and Populist Policies in Latin America." NBER Working Paper 2,897, National Bureau of Economic Research, Cambridge, MA.

Schiff, Maurice, and Alberto Valdes. 1992. *The Political Economy of Agricultural Pricing Policy: A Synthesis of the Economics in Developing Countries.* Baltimore and London: Johns Hopkins University Press for the World Bank.

Schultz, T. Paul. 1997. "Inequality in the Distribution of Personal Income in the World: How Is It Changing and Why?" Yale University. Mimeo.

Stallings, Barbara, ed. 1995. *Global Change, Regional Response: The New International Context of Development.* New York: Cambridge University Press.

Summers, Robert, and Alan Heston. 1995. "The Penn World Tables, Mark 5.6." University of Pennsylvania, Department of Economics. Mimeo.

United Nations Development Program. 1994. *Human Development Report, 1994.* New York: Oxford University Press.

World Bank. 1993. *The East Asian Miracle: Economic Growth and Public Policy.* Washington, DC: World Bank.

————. 1996. *World Development Report, 1996.* New York: Oxford University Press.

PART II

Social Policies and Income Distribution in a Rapid-Growth Setting

The Case of Chile

CHAPTER 7

Economic Growth, Social Equity, and Globalization: The Chilean Case

Eduardo Aninat

The main topic of this chapter is how to make modern economic growth patterns more compatible with the goals of equity, income distribution, and social justice that are aspired to by all societies on the path to equitable development. The subject is of utmost importance in the agenda of Chile's second reconciliation government and the agendas of virtually all developing countries. Today a debate is going on in the meetings of the Group of Seven countries, in Europe, and in the election process in the United States, which points in the same direction. What is happening to growth? What is happening to the modern economic model and its effects on income distribution? This is a subject that affects more than a few nations; it affects us all.

Growth, Inequality, and the Quality of Life

We know from experience that economic growth is essential for raising the standard of living and the quality of life by providing adequate amounts of new goods and services for consumers, workers, and families. We have learned from very painful experiences in the past that it is senseless to simply redistribute poverty, and many of the countries in the region, including Chile, have found that experimenting with populist policies and quick fixes for macroeconomic growth meant to spur rapid consumerism in the short term lead to backlashes that have a detrimental effect on income distribution. The recent painful experiences of countries such as Mexico and Argentina lend credence to the last point. The stagnation that normally follows cycles of strong but unsustainable growth is generally paid for by the poorest groups in every society. Economic growth is essential for reducing poverty through job creation and better quality jobs.

Chile in the 1990s has made major progress in terms of the number (and the percentage) of individuals who have been climbing out of poverty, as measured by traditional indicators. And among the poor there is also a significant percentage whose distance from the poverty line has narrowed. In the last five years, over a million people have moved to a higher level of well-being. This is undoubtedly related to the high average economic growth (close to 7 percent per year) in Chile during the last decade. The reduction in poverty has also been facilitated by social policies designed and administered by the government and focused particularly on the poorest and most marginalized sectors of the population. However, we are aware that much remains to be done.

How and to what extent can economic growth and more equitable income distribution become complementary objectives? How can the mutual relationship between equity and growth be strengthened? This chapter examines the experiences of other countries and regions in this crucial area. It is important to learn how social equity progresses in the different stages of economic development and during the evolution of per capita income and the qualitative changes brought on by that development. What has happened to the famous U curve we all studied, which was devised by the eminent Nobel laureate in economics, Simon Kuznets. Is the U curve being displaced? Has it been altered by technological change in the latter part of the century? What new patterns can be discovered? What concrete instruments and mechanisms can we use to ensure that faster development in Latin America and other regions will be coupled with greater social equity, equality, certainty, and speed? How can public policies help? One germane area of public policy is education, specifically work force skills and labor training. Education is an issue that Eduardo Frei's government has placed at the top of the agenda in its six-year program. We are launching a major educational reform, and we believe that many of its aspects will foster equity in the economic system. I will return to this subject at the end of the chapter.

What does recent economic history teach us about the mix of factors that permit rapid growth while simultaneously improving equity under the current model? One thing we know—and our people know even better, as the political system has found—is that economic development is incomplete. It wobbles like a table missing a leg or a building whose foundations are not strong enough if it does not lead toward greater social equity and the income distribution that society considers more acceptable and reasonable. The United Nations has been devising and disseminating a concept of human development that has a new way of combining economic and social indicators to measure progress in the quality of life. Chile is moving up in this new rating compared with its position in past years according to the United Nations' *Human Development Report*. The human development index seeks to apply in a more modern form elements that have been present in the literature on applied economics for several decades. I recall the social accounting matrix exercises that were carried out in a number of academic centers—for example, the advances that the International Labor Organization (ILO) prompted in the early 1970s through its basic needs approach. Much of this is reflected in the *Human Development Reports*. I recall the social progress indicators that ECLAC promoted. And I also recall the factors that institutions such as the World Bank, the Inter-American Development Bank (IDB), and the International Monetary Fund have discovered and are bringing to the table to round out our tools for measuring factors of this kind more accurately and precisely.

The goal is to understand how the quality of life is evolving across the entire social spectrum. The concept of quality of life includes public services and cultural goods, education levels, and life expectancy, and it goes beyond the caricature of a "homo economicus"—a fragmentary construct that is measured only by what it consumes in the formal market. That narrow view fails to take account of the environmental degradation caused by growth in the general habitat, the depletion of natural resources, overcrowding, and marginalization. The theme of sustainable growth thus also bears on the theme of social equity in the broad sense of the term.

The Savings and Investment Capacity of Poor Families

The focus in other chapters of this book on the potential of poor families and microentrepreneurs, who live on the edges of marginalization and poverty, to contribute to savings and investment is an interesting one. In Chile, where we have also been exploring this potential in our public policies, two examples come to mind. One interesting experience has been in low-cost housing, an area in which Chile has been making progress in the application of public policies clearly focused on the most vulnerable or marginal sectors, to which a broader approach to providing community facilities has been added. It is not simply a question of providing housing for needy groups but also of considering that the poor, too, have some capacity for savings. They know their own needs much better than do technocrats or bureaucrats. Another very successful experiment in Chile, which is of recent implementation, has been participatory urban paving projects, which are organized through the government in conjunction with low-income community groups. These groups have been asked to contribute between 15 and 85 percent of the cost of paving the sidewalks and streets used by teenagers, children, and workers. The project has been highly successful. There has been a kind of identification, a sense of the community ability to get things done and attract small savings to supplement the main work of government, which is leading to rapid changes in the habitat of these groups. The new educational reform is also making use of the idea of the organized community, of going to the grass roots, to the microeconomy of marginal groups, to foster self-help and the self-mobilization of resources and assistance in order to satisfy basic needs.

Fiscal Policy

This chapter also discusses fiscal policy, particularly the contribution of tax policy to the achievement of greater equity in development. This, of course, is a very relevant topic for ministers of finance. First, there is a macroeconomic dimension to fiscal policy. The issue of basic macroeconomic balance in the context of growth and the balance between private and public sector spending and its evolution over time is crucial. From the standpoint of equity, one of the most regressive taxes, which has always been hard on the very poor, is the so-called inflation tax. During the 1990s, Latin America has made extraordinary progress in this area in comparison with the 1960s, the 1970s, and much of the 1980s. In Latin America, the substantial reduction in inflation is having a very positive effect on equity. The effects are silent, unspectacular, and lacking pomp and circumstance, but surveys, other governments, and the Chilean government can very clearly see the positive effect that price stabilization has had on the basic consumption capacity of the population.

This is an aspect that should not be ignored. Fiscal austerity has made it possible to move from deficits to balances and then to fiscal savings, which in Chile stand at close to 5 percent of GDP. It is worth noting, too, that in Chile the government is a net contributor to the pool of economic savings. The makeup of the public budget, the way in which it is spent, and its focus, instruments, and distribution among the regions are also important considerations. It is here, I believe, that public servants have a real obligation. I remember one professor at Harvard who always said: "Well, we should be careful about exaggerating the effects of certain fiscal policies because one dollar in the hands of government bureaucrats is the equivalent, at most, of 10 cents for the end users of social spending." Public servants have the obligation to turn this equation around; no more than 10 or 15 cents should be spent on administration, bureaucracy, or the allocation of these resources; 85 or 90 cents should go directly to the beneficiaries of social spending. There has been great progress in Latin America in this area, as countries—some to a greater and some to a lesser extent—have learned how to use modern budget administration techniques in the social evaluation of projects. This has made it possible to focus spending better, reducing past leakages and unintended redistribution to groups that did not need such transfers.

International Trade, Technical Progress, and Income Distribution

One major topic on the agenda is the opening up to international trade of small and medium-sized countries, such as ours, which are still on the way to economic integration into macromarkets. We must study the impact of trade in goods and services and flows of foreign investment on growth and income distribution. For Chile, this is of the utmost importance. Direct foreign investment in sectors such as mining, fisheries, forestry, and agroindustry have macroeconomic and redistributional effects that must be gauged. Chile's membership in Mercado Comun del Sur (MERCOSUR), its possible integration with Canada and Mexico, and our participation in Asian-Pacific Economic Council (APEC) and the European Union will have effects on equity that we must visualize and plan for immediately. The traditional theories of international trade are useful, but they must be modified in a context of intense globalization, a true silent revolution in technology, and the global village. The revolution has affected the telecommunications industry, highly specialized services, finance, banking, cutting-edge technology, communications, and transportation. This brings to the fore the issue of mobility in productive factors, particularly in the case of financial and physical capital, which is far more relevant than could have been foreseen in the past. What happens to work under these conditions? What are the qualifications required to absorb these new trade flows, and what happens to distribution of the income derived from them? We know that the idea of technological change and higher productivity lies at the heart of economic growth that is sustainable over the long term. The distributional impact of technological change is an old topic that has taken on a new face. It is as old as the writings of the great English economist David Ricardo, who was interested in the subject. The impact of technological change on savings in the use of different kinds of labor—which affects workers in modernized industries—cannot be overlooked. The way in which the fruits of technological change are distributed between the owners of capital, managers, and workers is also crucial.

Finally, in my opinion the best response in this field is not to wall off technological change or globalization. The response is to work to understand it and design appropriate activities to absorb it, so that it will benefit workers in the broad sense and society as a whole. Here, we return to the issues of education, transformation of the productive sectors, and retraining as tools that governments and societies can use to facilitate the contribution that technical change can make to social welfare. On a more general level, the absorption and distributional impact of technical change is related to the labor market, the bargaining power of unions, the type of labor legislation in effect, and the balance in companies between the capital and labor factors.

Educational Reform in Chile: Macrofinancial Dimensions

I would now like to comment on the Frei government's educational reform as a fundamental mechanism for promoting social equity, equal opportunity, and economic growth.

In August 1994, during his first year in office, President Frei and his team set a major quantitative goal for spending and investments in education as a percentage of total GDP; achieving this goal by the year 2000, the end of this government's mandate, is a priority. The overall goal is to consolidate public and private spending on education at 7 percent of GDP. In 1994, the figure stood at about 4.5 percent of GDP in Chile, a country that has always attached great importance to education. In a rapidly growing country, raising the rate from 4.5 to 7 percent over a period of five or six years is no minor task. Today, the central government, the central fiscal apparatus, is expending close to U.S.$2.2 billion a year on the education system, not counting additional minor costs; this sum represents close to one-seventh of the total adjusted national budget.

What is the idea behind the educational reform discussed in greater detail and depth in the chapter by Sergio Molina? The idea in education is to move from the classical objectives of providing coverage at all levels in the system to improving its quality. Chile has already made great strides in educational coverage. The young people enrolled in private and public schools today need a change in the quality of their education and a fresh look at the objectives of the educational system to bring it abreast of human resource needs in a country undergoing rapid modernization and growth. The last educational reform in Chile took place in the 1960s. The country is very different today.

The new reform, a very ambitious plan that will be implemented in stages, is also aimed at mobilizing the agents of the current private and public education system: school principals; families; parents and guardians; teachers and professors; universities (in their role as educators of teachers); Chilean municipalities, which play a key role in managing much of the public educational system; and private educators. Indeed, the two core areas of primary and secondary education today are municipal education, which is subsidized by the government on a broad scale throughout the country, and private education, which also receives state support. Together, they account for about 90 percent of the system's coverage. The idea, developed by the Ministry of Education in conjunction with the Ministry of Finance, is to seek decentralized yet clearly regulated mechanisms that will change support formats for teachers and students with an eye to raising standards and the quality of the system. Action will be taken on two levels. First, the need to provide physical infrastructure for the school system, classrooms, and physical support will be addressed, a process that is expected to take from four to five years. Second, a system will be introduced to extend the school day in primary and secondary schools, which is a core element in the reform. The increase in the hours of schooling varies depending on the different primary and secondary school grades, but the percentages are significant and are linked to improvements in quality. A team of experts from the Ministry of Education, together with foreign experts who are familiar with the Chilean system, has concluded that the quality of the educational system cannot be improved without lengthening the school day. Currently, pupils in unsubsidized private primary education are at school between seven and eight hours a day, while most students in the subsidized system (public and private) are only in the classroom for four or five hours. This represents a very large differential in the quantity and quality of education in the two subsystems, with adverse effects on equality of opportunity in Chilean society.

In terms of financial resources, we are talking about an effort to provide an improved physical infrastructure, which includes more than classrooms, on the order of slightly more than U.S.$1 billion over a four-year transition period that began in 1997. During the transition, an additional $400 to $500 million in support will be made available for extension and teaching services and specific programs for professors and teachers. Once the system has become permanent, the investments in physical infrastructure have been made, and the new programs and support mechanisms are in place, long-term spending will average around $250 million a year. These funds will go toward increasing subsidies and supporting the extension of the school day in municipal systems and the subsidized private system.

I would like to stress three of the many avenues for financing the transition: (1) direct support from increased tax revenues stemming from growth in GDP; (2) net donations from the private sector, companies, foundations, and private organizations through a system of tax exemptions; and (3) reallocations and the assignment of new priorities in the budget. In the long term, our idea is to maintain the current level of support for the Chilean public education system if public finances continue to remain sound. Revenues from the value added tax VAT will be used to maintain the permanent system after the transition period has ended.

In economic terms, what we are proposing is an exchange of current consumption for investment in human capital through education, which will have medium- and long-term effects on individual productivity and income. The proposed reform, as described in the chapter by Sergio Molina, has a strong redistributional content. Preliminary studies on the impact of the package suggest that for each five dollars spent in net benefits for the poorest groups, those groups will contribute about one dollar in indirect financing for the system.

In short, our proposed educational reform makes a direct investment in Chile's growth potential and seeks to improve income distribution over the long term, in a more sustainable fashion, correcting present inequalities in opportunity for children and adolescents in a country that is very young. The reform also seeks to correct shortcomings in the quality of education in terms of repeater rates, outmoded curricula, dropout rates among children from low-income families, and the scant involvement of parents, guardians, and the community. We are not expecting a revolution, but we believe that the proposed reform will strengthen economic growth. If we are successful, it will improve long-term distribution profiles in Chile.

CHAPTER 8

Distribution and Poverty in Chile Today: Have We Gained or Lost Ground?

Kevin Cowan and José De Gregorio

Social issues and the question of equity are moving increasingly to the forefront of Chilean public debate. Six years into the nation's strategy of growth with equity, and in the wake of a recent CASEN survey,[1] many critical voices are making themselves heard. In some quarters, the strategy is faulted for poor design and incongruity and for failing to bring about substantive improvement in the standard of living of Chile's neediest. To these critics, most of the gains scored in the war on poverty can be attributed to the growth of the economy. Heavier public spending and higher taxes, they argue, have done nothing to improve the lives of the truly disadvantaged and, indeed, have worsened their lot, to the extent that the measures themselves are slowing economic growth. One might conclude from the press's perspective on this issue that the key is to foster growth and then wait for the benefits to trickle down to ordinary citizens. The second chorus of critics, their tone patently pessimistic, questions whether economic advances are being felt at all by the general population. As proof, they point to income distribution figures, "equity" being associated with a more equal sharing of monetary income. The apparent absence of a major shift in distribution over the past five years confirms, in their view, that the growth with equity strategy has led nowhere. The unremittingly pessimistic hold that the economic model and policy are incapable of bringing about the improvements the nation needs and that the present economic system requires far more deep-seated, structural changes.

Any constructive debate on this issue requires first a careful analysis of what the figures really tell us. In this chapter we examine current distributional and social conditions in Chile, trends in recent years, and medium-range prospects and attempt to broaden the framework of the discussion on social progress to take in more than simple household income distribution. An explanation of the array of economic, cultural, and historical factors that have brought Chile to its current distribution situation would exceed the scope of the chapter.

To begin with, economic and social progress, and the issue of equity generally, can be divided into two spheres. The first looks at income "levels" and living conditions that apply to the population at large. The issue of poverty figures prominently in this first sphere, having less to do with distributional concerns than with the level of income of the nation's less advantaged groups and with satisfying their basic needs. The second broad area has to do with distribution. It offers at least three dimensions: (1) income distribution, (2) distribution of consumption or spending levels, and (3) equality of opportunity. We propose to describe and graph the social gains posted to date by Chile in both the income-level and distributional spheres and within the latter to examine specifically the distribution of income and of expenditure.

In Chile, there exists (or there is some move to instill) a perception that the benefits of development are being felt by select sectors of the population, leaving the others to languish, and hand in hand with this perception is the impression that this state of affairs has triggered some measure of discontent and disquiet. The authors wish to make clear at the outset that the chapter will offer no explanation of such perceptions or apparent discrepancies between the prevailing climate and the figures. Our objective is more basic: to analyze the figures and, from such analysis, to portray the distributional situation and living conditions in Chile today.

Listed below, by way of a summation, are the principal propositions that the chapter will attempt to prove, which can also be viewed as its conclusions. They correspond in order to the various sections into which the chapter has been divided.

P.1. Income distribution in Chile is mediocre by international standards. To judge from the historical data available to the authors, this is a traditional feature of Chile's economy.

P.2. Income distribution gains are coming slowly, and no significant gains are likely for at least five years. For this reason, any realistic analysis in the future will have to forego an obsession with short-run movements in income distribution figures to avert the depressions that are triggered, and will continue to be triggered, with the release of each new set of CASEN survey findings.

P.3. The slight widening of cash income distribution between 1992 and 1994 is largely of cyclical origin; it does not denote a structural trend. The worsening of income distribution over this interval can be explained by the fact that 1992 marked the peak of the economic cycle, while in 1994 the economy was emerging from an adjustment process. Controlling for the effect of unemployment and informal occupation, income distribution in fact improved slightly between 1992 and 1994.

P.4. Fiscal policy, as translated into public spending on education and health services, is increasingly offsetting unequal income distribution. The richest 20 percent of Chileans receive roughly 13 times more cash income than the poorest 20 percent, but when the impact of social spending is factored in the ratio drops below 9. Assuming no change in targeting from 1992 to 1994, the exact figure is 8.6, down from 9 in 1990.

P.5. Impressive gains have been scored in the fight against poverty. The sustained reduction in the ranks of the poor in Chile is the fruit of sound economic growth in tandem with economic and social policies. What is more, these gains are being achieved more efficiently. In 1987–90, with every one-point rise in GDP growth the poverty rate fell only 0.2 points; in 1990–94, the reduction doubled to 0.4 points. If economic growth continues to be robust, by the year 2000 only 17 percent of the population may be living in poverty and only 3 percent in extreme poverty. Tempting as it might be to point to economic growth as the driving factor in poverty reduction, it is generally accepted that the advancement of an economy is tied to the quality of economic and social policies pursued against an orderly social and economic backdrop that is conducive to sound economic expansion. For that reason, we would eschew any distinction that pits "growth only" against "other factors only" to explain social progress; from a technical standpoint, any such attempt will necessarily entail a recourse to arbitrary assumptions.

P.6. Impressive gains have been made in social areas as well. Quality of life indicators for Chile have improved notably, and its position internationally is far stronger than a simple comparison of income distribution figures might lead one to believe.

From the evidence presented in the chapter, we would conclude that it is unrealistic to look only at income distribution — the traditional yardstick — to gauge the success of an economic and social policy, since changes are often imperceptible in the short or medium run and since, of the several dimensions of equity, income distribution is perhaps the least reachable by means of direct policies. Income distribution, in sum, is but one dimension of economic development. To zero in on that one factor is to ignore other objectives of social policy such as closing the opportunity gap, reducing poverty, raising the standard of living of the populace at large, and dispensing aid to those most in need.

Income distribution and the impact of fiscal policy on the distribution of expenditures are examined in the following two sections. Then the issue of levels in socioeconomic progress, that is, gains made in poverty reduction and improvements in other indicators that depict the quality of life of a people, is looked at. Concluding remarks are presented at the end of the chapter.

Income Distribution

Income Distribution in Chile: A Historical and International Perspective

Per capita income in Chile was 24 percent higher, on average, in 1994 than in 1990, but the income distribution changed very little over that interval (table 8.1). For corroboration, we have examined three indices typically used to measure a nation's distribution picture. The first, the Gini coefficient, is an approximate measure of the gap between actual and a uniform distribution. The Gini scale ranges from zero (perfect equality — income evenly spread across quintiles) to unity (total inequality): the higher the Gini coefficient, the more unequal the distribution. A second commonly used index is the income share of middle–lower middle income positions, that is, the share of the second and middle quintiles in total income, abbreviated herein as MID. The third measure

TABLE 8.1. Income Distribution per Household

Quintile	1990	1992	1994	2000[a]
1	4.2	4.8	4.5	5.2
2	8.8	8.6	8.3	9.1
3	12.9	12.3	12.1	12.6
4	19.0	18.3	18.2	17.9
5	55.1	56.0	56.9	55.2
B-T (5/1)	13.1	11.7	12.6	10.6
MID (2 + 3)	21.7	20.9	20.4	21.7
Gini	0.448	0.448	0.459	0.435

Source: CASEN surveys 1992 and 1994.

Note: 1990 data have not been adjusted for recent changes in the National Account series. The definition of income does not include provisions for house ownership. The Gini statistic is an approximation based on quintile data.

[a]2000 corresponds to a differentiated growth exercise (see text).

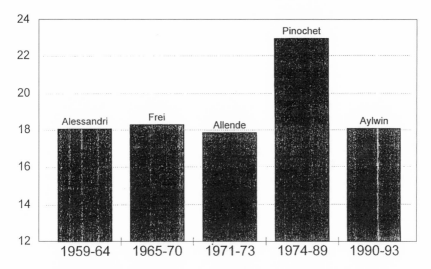

Fig. 8.1.   Evolution of income distribution: B-T for Chile, 1960–93. (From Marcel and Solimano 1994.)

is the ratio of bottom to top quintile income, which we abbreviate as B-T. Between 1992 and 1994, all three of these indices declined. The trend between 1990 and 1994 was slightly better or slightly worse, depending on the measure selected. Though different methodologies were used in the various CASEN surveys (and 1990 data, in particular, do not readily lend themselves to comparison with the new national accounts), the income distribution would appear to have been virtually stationary between 1990 and 1994.

According to historical data drawn from standardized University of Chile surveys of greater Santiago (see Marcel and Solimano 1994), there has been little shift in the distribution in the long term either. The changes recorded from one presidential administration to the next, except in 1974–89 (fig. 8.1), are minimal; this is all the more striking when one considers the variety of economic orders in place over these more than 30 years. This lends credence to the argument that income distribution is tied most of all to structural factors, which are exceedingly difficult to alter in the short run.

Figure 8.2 graphs Chile's status vis-à-vis selected countries in terms of income distribution and growth. The horizontal axis shows the ratio of income of the bottom of the top quintile (B-T); the vertical axis plots average growth in per capita GDP from 1980 to 1993.

A word of caution is in order before analyzing these figures. Since

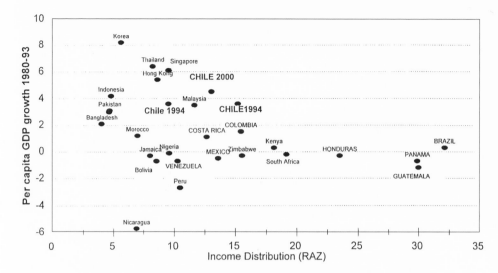

Fig. 8.2.   Growth and distribution: Developing countries. (Adapted from World Bank 1995; Chilean Central Bank; authors' estimates based on CEPAL 1995; and Chilean Ministry of Finance statistics.) *Note:* Income distribution refers to the B-T variable described in the text. Countries in capital (or lowercase) letters refer to personal distribution of income (consumption). CHILE 1994 is the personal distribution of income in Chile according to CEPAL 1995. CHILE 2000 is a differentiated growth scenario described in the text. Chile 1994 is a first approach to the distribution of consumption since it includes public social expenditure.

cross-country comparisons are rarely precise, care must be taken with any conclusions drawn from them.[2] One immediate comparability problem is whether to measure income distribution looking at individuals or at households. Since poorer households are larger, per capita distribution figures tend to be more unequal than household ones.[3] Specifically, the poorest quintile of households in Chile received 4.6 percent of total income in 1994, whereas the poorest quintile of individuals received only 3.6 percent of the total. And the wealthiest quintile of households received 56.1 percent of overall income, while the richest quintile of individuals received 60.3 percent of the total. This explains the main differences between the Chile data presented in the World Bank's 1995 *World Development Report* (based on individuals) and the CASEN figures (which are based on households), even though the data source is the same.

A further major distinction to bear in mind in cross-country comparisons is whether the data refer to income or consumption (expenditure).

Two elements prepare one to expect greater inequality in income distribution than in the distribution of consumption. First, the higher the income, the higher is the percentage of income not consumed (i.e., the higher the saving ratio). Hence, the lion's share of saving is generated by upper income sectors, and consumption thus would tend to be spread more evenly. Second, to the extent that consumption that is publicly funded (public education and health care, for instance) can be accounted for, and to the extent that fiscal policy is targeted to the neediest,[4] consumption would likewise tend to be more evenly distributed than income. Country names in lower case in figure 8.2 denote expenditure data; for those in upper case, income data are used. With these reservations, a cross-country comparison can be done to portray Chile's standing.

To judge from income distribution figures based on CASEN (CHILE 1994), Chile's impressive economic growth has not been matched by improvements in income distribution; its performance on this front can only be termed undistinguished (fig. 8.2). However, as will become apparent later, the picture changes substantially for the better when one looks at distribution of expenditure rather than distribution of income (CHILE 1994).

To what extent can the income distribution really be improved? Let us imagine a "structural" income distribution that is the average of the 1992 and 1994 distributions, assume that this distribution continued to hold in late 1995,[5] and then perform the following exercise. Assume a scenario of progressive distribution with 1996 economic growth of 6.5 percent across all income positions. Assume next that the economy continues to grow, on average, by 6 percent annually until 2000, but at different rates in the different income percentiles, with a gradual improvement in income distribution (assume 9 percent growth for the bottom quintile, 8 percent for the second, and 7 percent for the middle). Meanwhile, the upper two quintiles grow on a par with aggregate growth. The last column in table 8.1 (2000) presents the results of this simulation. While the income share of the poorest does increase by the end of 2000, the gain is hardly impressive, and presumably few would be elated by it.[6] As graphed in figure 8.2, which presents this simple simulation (called CHILE 2000) in an international context, Chile's standing vis-à-vis the rest of the world changes very little.

The foregoing figures would confirm propositions P.1 and P.2. Given the limitations described, income distribution in Chile has been, and is, mediocre by international standards. Moreover, such changes as have been achieved have been very slow in coming, as figures for past decades and the simulation findings both attest, so there is little likelihood of any fundamental change in the next four or five years. The country will need sustained, differentiated growth if any definitive gains are to be made on this front. Obviously, then, to examine equalization trends and gauge the success of Chilean social policy in the recent past, we will need to look beyond income distribution.

It would be no easy task to pinpoint the key determinants of unequal distribution of income in Chile, and this essay does not propose to do so. Nevertheless, it is important to note that unequal income distribution is something of a constant in Latin America, and a series of common elements, born of decades if not centuries of economic development, go some way toward explaining this structural feature of the region's economies.

The 1992–94 Backslide

There is no question that income distribution worsened, albeit slightly, between 1992 and 1994. During that interval, per capita income in the lowest decile fell by 3.9 percent, from Ch$11,582 to Ch$11,131 in November 1994 currency. Why did this happen? Was it associated with a structural phenomenon of widening inequality or was it cyclical? And must we then conclude that the "growth with equity" strategy has been a failure? We propose in this section to show that the 1992–94 slippage in distribution and the decline in income in the bottom decile are related phenomena, rooted essentially in the economic cycle and with only a tenuous connection to structural changes; they therefore do not bespeak a failure of national economic and social policy or of the economic order generally.

While the country boasted strong economic performance throughout the 1990–94 period, it is important to remember that, in terms of business cycle stages, circumstances in late 1994 bore scant resemblance to 1992. In 1992, Chile's economy soared, with second-half GDP growth of 11.8 percent. The picture was altogether different in 1994, as the economy emerged from a period of adjustment and posted a second-half rise in output of only 4.3 percent. Unemployment for the quarter ending November 1992 (the month of the 1992 CASEN survey) stood at 4.8 percent, well below the 6.5 percent reported for the corresponding period two years later.

There is an international body of evidence to explain how income distribution is affected by the economic cycle and short-run fluctuations in activity and inflation.[7] For one thing, inflation takes its heaviest toll on low-income groups, which are the least well equipped to protect themselves against losses in purchasing power. The same studies underscore the importance of the level and quality of employment in passing from activity fluctuations to income distribution.[8] In the case of Chile, Marcel and Solimano (1994) found a rise in unemployment rates to be one of the key triggers of a loss in income share in the poorest quintiles. From this, it would follow that distributional disparities and falling income of the poorest groups between 1992 and 1994 can be ascribed in large measure to the following labor market changes.

Unemployment. Unemployment is highest among those with the lowest incomes — a condition that is hardly unique to Chile and indeed prevails throughout South America (table 8.2). To some extent, this is a tautology: the unemployed, by definition, have no employment earnings, so in the poorer segments of society there will be higher numbers of jobless. By the same token, temporary rises in unemployment mean more jobless persons in the lower quintiles. For instance, a second-quintile worker who loses his job may slip into the bottom quintile, thereby pushing up the numbers of the unemployed among low-income groups.[9] Consequently, the income of the poorest does not fall simply because there is greater unemployment at their income position but also because their ranks are swelled when people formerly in a higher quintile find themselves without jobs.[10] It thus comes as no surprise that unemployment in the bottom quintile climbed from 18 percent to 22 percent between 1992 and 1994.

TABLE 8.2. **Unemployment by Income Group**

Country	Year	Total	First Quintile (1)	Fifth Quintile (2)	Unemployment Distribution (1)/(2)
Chile	1987	10.9	26.5	2.7	9.8
	1994	6.8	17.9	2.0	9.0
Argentina	1986	6.6	24.3	1.3	18.7
	1992	6.7	18.6	1.2	15.5
Bolivia	1992	5.5	16.6	1.9	8.7
Brazil	1990	4.5	11.9	1.4	8.5
Colombia	1986	13.1	27.4	3.8	7.2
	1992	9.1	19.7	3.0	6.6
Costa Rica	1992	4.2	15.5	0.6	25.8
Honduras	1992	5.1	11.3	1.4	8.1
Mexico	1992	4.3	7.1	2.8	2.5
Panama	1986	12.4	23.1	2.4	9.6
	1991	18.6	35.2	6.1	5.8
Paraguay	1992	5.0	13.5	1.8	7.5
Uruguay	1986	9.0	18.4	2.9	6.3
	1992	8.4	15.9	3.0	5.3
Venezuela	1986	11.3	33.4	2.4	13.9
	1992	7.3	26.0	1.4	18.6

Source: CEPAL 1995.

Quality of salaried employment and the rise in informal occupation. A second feature of the labor market that drives down the income share of the poor during intervals of sluggish economic growth is the increase in informal occupation and the deterioration in work conditions this entails.

According to CASEN figures, the percentage of salaried workers earning less than the minimum wage jumped from 48 percent in 1992 to 67 percent in 1994. Apart from greater unemployment, there evidently was a reduction in hours worked per employee. This explains why the per capita income of salaried workers in the bottom decile rose during that period by barely 1.8 percent while the minimum wage went up by 11.7 percent. Furthermore, every class of worker saw a rise in real wages between 1992 and 1994. Nonspecialized workers' wages, for instance (the least-skilled wage earners), climbed 11 percent between November 1992 and November 1994, outstripping the per capita growth rate of the economy. Executives and professionals, along with clerical workers and sales personnel, earned 10 percent more. Skilled workers came in for the lowest increase, 7 percent.

Wage earners in the bottom decile accounted for 83 percent of the employed in that income position in 1992 but only 75 percent in 1994. This drop — this increase in the ranks of the self-employed — pushed down per worker earnings, since the average income of the self-employed in the lowest decile is only 67 percent of what their salaried counterparts make. Furthermore, in contrast to bottom decile employment earnings, which moved up between 1992 and 1994, the average income of the self-employed in the same interval dropped by 1.5 percent.

One simple way to quantify the effect of changes in employment and informal occupation on the income distributions is to take the distribution of household employment earnings for 1992 and then progressively adjust each variable that changed between that year and 1994 to isolate the effects of each change on the income distribution. The outcome of such an exercise is presented in table 8.3. Line 2 is the income-distribution calculation assuming 1992 decile unemployment rates identical to actual 1994 rates. For this scenario, the table presents a B-T ratio of 12 rather than the 11.7 that was actually the case with a lower unemployment rate.[11] This first scenario isolates the negative effect of higher unemployment rates on the income distribution. Line 3 of the table presents the distribution calculated by aggregating, to the aforementioned change, changes in the composition of employment between salaried workers and the nonsalaried (self-employed and low-income persons working informally). As this line indicates, the combination of larger ranks of informal workers and higher unemployment widens the distribution, as portrayed in higher Gini coefficients and B-T ratios and lower MIDS. The next line aggregates the change in average income of the self-employed following a reduction in number of hours worked, coupled with deteriorating work conditions. With such a change, the 1992 income distribution — with an unemployment rate, a mix of salaried and self-employed workers, and self-employment earnings levels identical to 1994 — would have been worse than in 1994. To put it another way, the above-mentioned factors would more than explain the generalized worsening of income distribution between 1992 and 1994. As further confirmation, table 8.3 illustrates an improvement in the per worker wage distribution from 1992 to 1994. And this in turn supports our proposition P.3: decile changes in income in Chile from 1992 to 1994 can be ascribed essentially to the different sets of economic circumstances holding sway in each of those years. As unemployment and informal employment are reduced, the gains accruing to the poorest should be more noticeable; we assume that such will indeed prove to have been the case in 1995 against a backdrop of robust economic growth.

The foregoing discussion, apart from explaining the transitory nature of changes in income distribution, points up the importance for the nation's poor of access to good jobs if their lives are to improve. Simply put, if the earnings of a family head increase by 15 percent (a strong increase), the family's income will double in five years, whereas, if a second earner is added to a household that previously had only one, household income will double in only one year. This is why it is essential to produce conditions in which persons of few means can be equipped to enter the work force and secure jobs. All evidence to date shows that for the moment the participation rate of those in the poorest quintiles

TABLE 8.3.   Income Distribution and the Labor Market

	B-T	MID	Gini
Distribution of income from labor by household			
(1) 1992 Distribution	11.74	0.209	0.450
(2) Changes in unemployment	12.04	0.208	0.452
(3) Changes in informality	12.19	0.204	0.457
(4) Changes in income of informal worker	13.22	0.194	0.472
(5) 1994 Distribution	12.81	0.203	0.462
Distribution of wages per worker			
Wage income, 1992	5.76	0.246	0.350
Wage income, 1994	5.79	0.252	0.345

Source: Authors' calculations based on CASEN 1992 and 1994 surveys.

Note: Labor income = (wages) + income from independent work. Starting from the 1992 distribution, the table shows the effects of successively modifying the following parameters for each decile:

1. Unemployment rate → Changes in unemployment
2. Level of informality → Changes in informality
3. Income per informal worker → Changes in income of informal worker

is considerably lower than the economy average. In 1994, 42 percent of the country's indigent were part of the labor force compared with 56.6 percent in the more affluent sectors.

We thus are left with the following conclusions: in the poorer income positions, fewer people are seeking employment; fewer of those who *are* looking manage to find a job; and those who do have jobs have to maintain families that are larger, on average, than in the rest of the population. These three factors explain the 4.5 dependency ratio[12] in the bottom decile in 1994 — well above the national average of 2.9 — as well as the fact that average per capita income in the country generally is seven times higher than per capita bottom decile income. On the other hand, if we compare average income per wage earner, this ratio drops to 4. One factor that impacts very strongly on the dependency ratio in the different quintiles is female labor force participation. This issue was explored by Beyer (1995), who concludes that even with an improvement in distribution at the wage-earner level, as presented in table 8.3, the relatively faster entry of high-income women into the job market triggers a relative decline in household income distribution. According to Beyer, the lower participation rate of poor women is culturally based. In lower income groups, women leave the home to work only in cases of dire need, so any positive impact on the distribution that might ensue from a relative decline in unemployment or a relative increase in earnings at that income position would be offset in part by women leaving the labor force. This has very important implications for policy decisions. However much one might wish for a stronger female presence in the work force and a smoother distribution of income, there is no denying that this is a voluntary decision and would therefore entail an increase in the level of utility for the decision maker. This poses serious questions about the usefulness of income distribution figures when they are not controlled for changes in the gender stratification of the work force.

Fiscal Policy as an Instrument for Equity

Fiscal policy, as was noted earlier, indirectly affects income distribution and economic growth, but it also has direct effects on income, consumption, and personal opportunity. Its first and most obvious effect is the one achieved through cash grants or transfers, which form part of the recipient's total income package. Likewise, social policies that dispense goods and services (public health care, free education, basic infrastructure investment, and so on) supplement the income of those benefiting from such assistance. Carefully targeted social spending clearly can go some way toward equalizing consumption.[13]

Final figures on the impact of social spending in 1994 are not yet in; table 8.4 is an early approximation to the distribution of consumption.[14] It was assumed for purposes of this table that program targeting remained unchanged between 1992 and 1994 and hence that social spending on each decile rose at the same rate as total spending under that program.[15] On this basis, the average income accruing to each household decile from social programs was estimated and aggregated to 1994 CASEN data on total cash income.[16]

As illustrated in row II of table 8.4, one-third of cash grants go to the poorest quintile. While this helps even out the distribution, the improvement is slight because such transfers account for a minimal fraction of total income. In the bottom quintile in 1992, for instance, average cash transfers (such subsidies accounting for one-third of the total) were Ch$5,249 (1992 Chilean pesos), corresponding to 7.7 percent of mean income in that quintile.

Education and health programs have a more pronounced effect than cash subsidies. Over 80 percent of health care and 60 percent of educational services go to the poorest 40 percent of Chileans. Moreover, such programs also represent a larger share of total household spending. Consequently, while the wealthiest fifth of the population has just over 13 times more "own" income than those in the bottom quintile, the total is only 8.6 times greater after the impact of social spending is factored in. The distribution did worsen between 1992 and

TABLE 8.4.   The Effect of Social Expenditure (average monthly income per household, 1994, in percentages)

	Quintile					
Source of Income	1	2	3	4	5	5/1
I. Autonomous income	4.3	8.2	12.0	18.3	57.3	13.3
II. Monetary subsidies	33.4	27.8	19.6	13.1	6.1	0.2
III. Total monetary incomes						
(I + II)	4.5	8.3	12.1	18.2	56.9	12.6
IV. Social programs	39.1	28.3	20.0	10.4	2.2	0.1
Health	49.3	33.4	23.5	4.1	−10.3	−0.2
Education	34.8	26.2	18.5	13.1	7.5	0.2
V. Total income (III + IV)	6.3	9.4	12.5	17.8	54.0	8.6
Total income, 1990	5.9	9.8	13.2	18.6	52.5	8.9
Total income, 1992	6.4	9.9	13.2	18.3	52.1	8.1
Total income, 1994	6.3	9.4	12.5	17.8	54.0	8.6

Source: MIDEPLAN 1994; Ministry of Finance, Chile 1995.
Note: This table estimates the effect of social expenditure, assuming that focalization of expenditure remains unchanged between 1992 and 1994.

TABLE 8.5. Poverty Reduction

Country and Period	Annual Reduction of the Poor Population (%) (1)	Initial Poverty Level (2)	Average Yearly GDP Growth for the Period (3)	Yearly Fall in Poverty (%) (1)/(2)	Poverty Reduction per Point of GDP Growth (%) (1) × (3)/2
Chile (1987–94)	2.3	44.6	7.0	5.2	0.7
Indonesia (1970–87)	2.3	58.0	6.7	4.0	0.6
Malaysia (1973–87)	1.7	37.0	6.0	4.6	0.8
Brazil (1960–80)	1.5	50.0	8.3	3.0	0.4
Pakistan (1962–84)	1.4	54.0	4.2	2.6	0.6
Costa Rica (1971–86)	1.4	45.0	3.7	3.1	0.8
Colombia (1971–88)	0.9	41.0	4.4	2.2	0.5

Source: World Bank 1990.

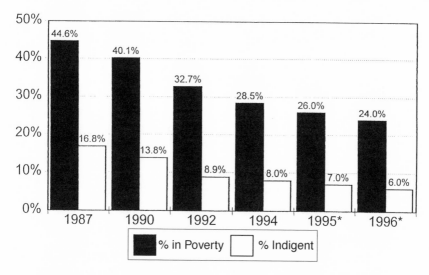

Fig. 8.3. Poverty (percentage of population). (Adapted from CEPAL 1995 and authors' estimates based on a fixed income distribution.)

1994, though the deterioration was less pronounced than in the case of "own" income. This suggests that heavier, targeted, social spending did go some way toward cushioning the regressive impact of the 1994 adjustment. In sum, Chile's fiscal policy has helped raise the low incomes of its poor, confirming proposition P.4.

Beyond Distribution: Poverty and Living Conditions

Poverty

One area in which definite progress can be reported is poverty reduction. Table 8.5 and figure 8.3 depict gains posted on this front using the poverty-line approach.[17] Other measuring tools, be they modified forms of the basic poverty-line methodology[18] or income-based techniques,[19] likewise depict a definite easing of poverty in Chile between 1987 and 1994. Table 8.5 presents the outcome of selected poverty reduction exercises that the World Bank has deemed successful. We have added more recent figures for Chile, which at the time could boast of little success on that score. However, in the wake of the impressive strides documented in the 1990s, Chile now ranks among the nations in which poverty is being brought down most quickly.[20]

Notice that the time interval examined for Chile is shorter than the spans used for the other countries, and this could skew the comparison: it is more difficult, and thus more impressive, to reduce poverty systematically over a protracted period of time. Conversely, and as a bias in the other direction, poverty in all the other countries depicted, except Malaysia and Colombia, was worse than in Chile. It is relatively easier to lower the poverty rate by one percentage point starting from 50 percent than from 20 percent poverty. To take account of this element, the last two columns in table 8.6 present an "efficiency index" for poverty reduction that measures the percentage reduction in the fraction of individuals living in poverty for every one-point rise in GDP.

One drawback to the foregoing comparisons is that individual country figures are constructed on the basis of country-specific poverty thresholds. In an attempt to get around this problem, a number of studies have taken an identical poverty line (or lines) for all countries.[21] Table 8.7 presents the findings of Chen, Datt, and Ravallion (1994) for a sample of 41 developing countries and our own estimates for Chile based on the

TABLE 8.6.   Efficiency of Growth in Poverty Reduction

	% Change in		Growth	GDP Elasticity		Efficiency of Growth	
	Poor (1)	Very Poor (2)	GDP (%) (3)	Poor (1/3)	Very Poor (2/3)	Poor	Very Poor
1987–90	−4.5	−3.0	21.70	−0.21	−0.14	−0.46	−0.82
1990–92	−7.4	−4.9	19.10	−0.39	−0.26	−0.97	−1.86
1992–94	−4.2	−0.9	10.80	−0.39	−0.08	−1.19	−0.94

Source: CASEN 1994 and CASEN 1990 surveys, and Central Bank of Chile.

TABLE 8.7.   Poverty in Developing Countries

		Percentage of Population below Each Level of Consumption (U.S.$/person/month, PPP 1985)				
Region	Year	21	30.42	40	50	60
East Asia	1990	4.9	14.7	26.8	39.1	49.3
Latin America	1990	17.2	27.8	37.0	45.2	52.1
South Asia	1990	33.3	58.6	74.3	83.8	59.4
Sub-Saharan Africa	1990	33.4	52.9	65.6	74.1	80.0
Total (41 countries)	1990	17.8	33.5	46.4	57.0	64.8
Chile	1992	4.3	11.6	20.8	30.9	37.0

Sources: Chen, Datt, and Ravallion 1994 and authors' estimations based on CASEN 1990 survey.
Note: PPP = purchasing power parity.

1992 CASEN survey.[22] Their study depicts fractions of the population living below an income level common to all countries. It is clear from the table that in 1992 poverty was lower in Chile than in the other countries. The percentage of Chilean poor is, for one thing, substantially lower than the Latin American average and is likewise below the East Asian average.

Poverty rates came down more quickly in the 1990s than between 1987 and 1990, despite the lower initial levels in the 1990s (table 8.6). Moreover, the effect of growth on poverty reduction between 1992 and 1994 was as efficient as in 1990–92 and more efficient than in 1987–90. For every percentage point of increase in GDP between 1987 and 1990, the ranks of the poor shrank by 0.2 points; between 1990 and 1994, the improvement doubled, with a 0.4 point reduction in poverty for every one-point rise in output.

Initial poverty rates, once again, must be taken into account in calculations like these. A recalculation by subperiod of the figure in the last column in table 8.5 yields, for 1987–90, a 0.5 percentage point reduction in the fraction of poor households for every point of GDP growth; for 1990–92 and 1992–94, the reduction is at least doubled (1 and 1.2 percent, respectively).

Progress on eradicating extreme poverty was slower in 1992–94 than in the preceding two years. This lag is only to be expected, since extreme poverty is found in the bottom decile, where average income, as was discussed earlier, fell by 3.9 percent.[23]

Looking at all of the evidence, and with no need to hazard any radical assumptions as to economic performance, one might well ask what effect 8.5 percent growth would have on end of 1995 poverty levels. At the present time, for every one-point increase in GDP, between 50,000 and 60,000 people are rising out of poverty. Taking the 1994 income distribution as a given, the poverty trend can be forecast by varying average income at the rate of per capita GDP growth.[24] According to such an estimation, in a scenario of 6.5 percent growth in 1996, 24 percent of the population would still be below the poverty line at year's end and 6 percent would still live in extreme poverty. With continuing 6 percent growth, by the end of 2000 only 18 percent would be poor and 3.5 percent indigent. By that standard, poverty would be stamped out by 2006 and extreme poverty would be eradicated by 2019.

The information presented in this subsection confirms proposition P.5: Chile has made major progress toward poverty reduction. Assuming sustained growth and the requisite social policies, it is possible that by the turn of the century only 18 percent of Chileans will fall below the poverty threshold and 3.5 percent will continue in extreme poverty.

The Effects of Growth on Poverty Reduction:
A Digression

It will be clear from the figures cited above that economic growth is, and will continue to be, fundamental to the eradication of poverty. That being the case, a number of studies have sought to quantify this relationship. The basic tenet is that poverty is reduced in a nation when the income of those hitherto grouped below a poverty threshold moves above that line; by definition, then, poverty is reduced when the income of the poor rises.

To separate the effect of growth, some authors have proposed, grosso modo, a segregation of two components of increases in the income of the poor — one attributable to aggregate economic growth and the other to "other," that is, the additional increase in the income of the poor above and beyond that aggregate. This "other" implies a shift in the income distribution in an economy. Analyses along these lines have been done by Larrañaga (1994), who traced 80 percent of poverty reduction between 1987 and 1992 to growth in average per capita income.[25]

To understand this analytical approach, we can write growth in income of the poorest groups (g) as the sum of two components: aggregate growth (g_A) and growth above and beyond aggregate income (g_E).[26] Where g_E is other than zero, the income of the poorest will grow at a rate different from the economy average and the income distribution will shift.

However sound the foregoing analysis might be from an "accounting" standpoint, it often lends itself to errors of interpretation. The first misinterpretation is to associate g_A with trend-rate or hands-off economic growth and g_E with social policies. For one thing, social policies affect the aggregate growth of an economy, which can only be robust and sustainable in a climate of peace and social harmony, with a well-educated and healthy populace — such variables being strongly influenced by social policy.[27] In short, social policies (and, indeed, economic policy generally) affect g_A and g_E simultaneously. To analyze the overall effect of social policy on poverty, we would have to decompose the rise in income of the poorest not into g_A and g_E but into income growth that can truly be ascribed to social policies and the rest.

A second interpretation error is to fail to consider the relationship g_A and g_E themselves. A large body of literature on social development, pioneered by Kuznetz (1955), associates long-run income distribution trends and economic growth. But the distributional impact, in the short run, of the type of rapid growth that Chile has experienced in recent years is not well understood. Perhaps the dislocations in a number of sectors or regions during this interval, which admittedly have improved living conditions in the country, have also worsened the income distribution. To accept such a hypothesis would mean rethinking the parameters used to assess movements in income distribution in Chile. The apparent stagnation could then be put down to a combination of conditions that would have averted such a backslide in the distribution. Nevertheless, it would be a mistake to credit social policy alone for every shift in distribution and write off the effects of the growth process. And the inverse also holds true. Income distribution has an impact on growth; specifically, it has been found that a more equitable distribution can make for stronger growth.[28] Growth and distribution, then, are not mutually exclusive but related. And once that linkage is acknowledged the problem of distribution and growth is no longer how to enlarge the pie and then (separately) divide it. The issue needs to be addressed from a far broader perspective.

In the short run, when an economy is growing robustly and in equilibrium the growth rate is roughly the same across most sectors and the income distribution is slow to change. This makes it unlikely that with the above-posited decomposition for recent years the growth effect would turn out to have less of an influence than the redistribution effect. For instance, between 1992 and 1994, given the slight widening of the income distribution, such a decomposition would likely attribute more than 100 percent to the growth effect and a negative effect to "other." It would be fallacious to conclude from this exercise that social policies have hampered poverty reduction and that, accordingly, the better course would have been to do nothing on the social spending front.

This raises the question of whether g_E should, in fact, always be higher than zero. Which is to be preferred: 6 percent growth across the board or 2 percent growth with 6 percent growth for the poor? Poverty would be reduced at the same pace under either scenario, and in the second instance the redistribution effect might be given the credit for two-thirds of the poverty reduction, suggesting to some that the government's policy has been a resounding success. But who, if anyone, would advocate such a scenario?

Living Conditions

Beyond equity considerations, poverty levels are one important indicator of living conditions in a country. But there are other quality of life indicators that are closely tied to equal opportunity.

Basically, there are two broad approaches to poverty measurement. The first, which includes the techniques discussed earlier in this chapter, looks at household cash income. One limitation of this "poverty-line" approach is that a family's basic needs are not satisfied by money alone: it also needs access to government goods and services, free or subsidized education and health care, decent shelter, and basic infrastructure. From this standpoint, poverty measurement (like income distribution measurement) overlooks a huge social policy component. An alternative line of attack, which takes greater account of household consumption levels, is the "unmet basic needs" approach.[29] No current data from these techniques were available to the authors, but, as table 8.8 illustrates, the changes between 1990 and 1994 in variables that denote the satisfaction of basic needs (such as access to safe water, sewer systems, and electricity) point to a reduction in poverty defined in terms of basic human needs.

One pivotal consideration here is the quality of education in a nation and the percentage of the population with access to schooling. Education is at once an end and a means: as an end, it has direct implications for living conditions and personal opportunity, and as a means it is a way to enhance human capital and thereby brighten prospects for personal earnings and the country's economic advancement generally.[30] In figure 8.4, literacy rates and average years of schooling are compared for Chile and 20 other countries in 1992, to afford an aggregate picture. As this graph indicates, Chile's showing on both counts is among the best in Latin America: at this writing, for instance, roughly 80 percent of Chileans between the ages of 12 and 17 are enrolled in secondary school.

Good health care is a second sine qua non for improvements in living conditions and equal opportunity. Figure 8.5 assumes the life expectancy at birth of a Chilean in 1994 to be 74—one of the highest in Latin America. Likewise, infant mortality in Chile now stands at 11.8 per 1,000 live births, one of the lowest rates on record in the developing countries.

One measure that blends the above-mentioned considerations with per capita income to come up with an overall yardstick of national socioeconomic development status is the UNDP's human development

TABLE 8.8.   Basic Services

	1990 (%)	1994 (%)	% Change (1990–94)
Households with electricity	88.6	93.2	5.2
Households with sewerage	74.5	78.9	5.9
Households with running water	72.2	81.3	12.6
Coverage of preschool education	20.9	26.9	28.7
Coverage of primary education	96.8	97.6	0.8
Coverage of high school education	80.3	83.8	4.4

Source: MIDEPLAN, CASEN surveys 1990–94.

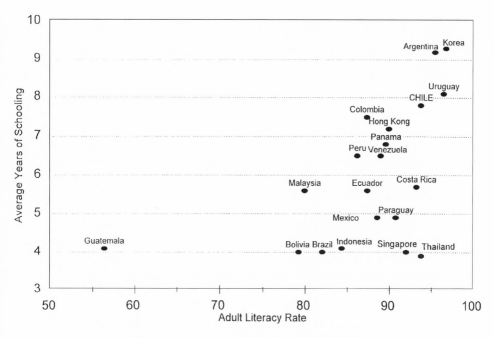

Fig. 8.4.   Education indicators. (From UNDP 1995.)

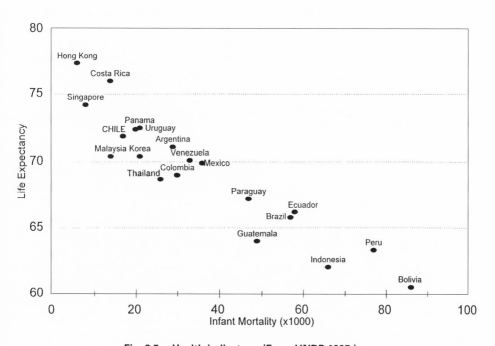

Fig. 8.5.   Health indicators. (From UNDP 1995.)

index, which is a composite indicator of life expectancy, educational attainment (literacy and enrollment ratios), and per capita income. The latest edition of the index places Chile among the 10 developing countries (of the 128 selected) with the best living conditions; when the industrialized nations are added to make the comparison international, Chile ranks thirty-third. One telling observation is that, when per capita income alone is compared, Chile slips downward in rank; this confirms that the country's positive social indicators have much to do with its strong performance (table 8.9).

The evidence offered in the preceding paragraphs confirms proposition P.6: living conditions in Chile are indeed improving, as the indicators attest, and those same indicators affirm that living conditions in Chile are better than income distribution measures may portray.

Concluding Remarks

As we have underscored in this chapter, there are at least three dimensions to the question of distribution: income, consumption, and opportunity. The implications of the latter two for economic policy decisions are self-evident: as a country upgrades its educational system and makes schooling available to more of the citizenry, gives more of its people access to health and other basic services, and dispenses social assistance to those genuinely in need, the entire population will be able to satisfy basic consumer needs and more and more of them will have the opportunity to raise their incomes.

Because income distribution patterns change slowly and income distribution is but one of a number of critical facets of socioeconomic progress, one may conclude that the success or failure of social policies should not be judged solely on the basis of improvements in income distribution. Such changes as do come about in the short run are cyclical rather than structural, and, though the structural changes are the lasting ones, they take a long time to instill. Improvements in education, for instance, take years to translate into significant improvements in income distribution. People who have benefited from an upgraded education system first have to make their way into the labor force, and many years will pass before they come to account for a major portion of it. The income distribution in Chile today, then, is the fruit not so much of current social policies as of a combination of social policy, education strategy, health programs, and other initiatives put in place over the past two or three decades, if not longer.

One key element in the issue of equity that warrants more in-depth analysis is the distribution of opportunities. Two extremes are possible in

TABLE 8.9. Human Development Index

County	Classification According to HDI	HDI	Classification According to GDP per Capita	Life Expectancy at Birth	Adult Literacy Rate (%)	Percentage of School Enrollment	GDP per Capita (PPP)
Canada	1	0.95	8	77	99	100	20.520
United States	2	0.94	1	76	99	95	23.760
Japan	3	0.94	9	80	99	77	20.520
Hong Kong	24	0.91	10	79	91	70	20.340
Bahamas	25	0.89	22	73	98	74	17.360
Costa Rica	28	0.88	60	76	94	66	5.480
Argentina	30	0.88	39	72	96	79	8.860
Korea	31	0.88	38	71	97	79	9.250
Uruguay	32	0.88	53	73	97	77	6.070
Chile	33	0.88	41	74	95	71	8.410
Malta	34	0.88	44	76	87	75	8.281
Singapore	35	0.88	16	75	90	68	18.330
Portugal	36	0.87	34	75	86	77	9.850
Brazil	63	0.80	64	66	82	70	5.240
High Human Development Countries		0.89		73	96	75	13.605
Peru	93	0.71	94	66	87	79	3.300
Ecuador	68	0.78	73	69	88	71	4.350
Paraguay	87	0.72	90	70	91	59	3.390
Bolivia	113	0.56	112	59	81	66	2.410
Intermediate Human Development Countries	—	0.63	—	67	79	59	2.631

Source: UNDP 1995.
Note: PPP = purchasing power parity.

a scenario of economies with identical distributions: (1) in one, those born into a certain social group are destined to remain there, and (2) in the other, personal ability and effort will determine the level of income to which individuals can aspire. However identical the income distribution in the two instances, the second society is evidently the more equitable one. Unfortunately, there are no data available to accurately measure changes in the distribution of opportunity in Chile. One would somehow have to calculate the likelihood that a child born into a poor family would be able to rise above those circumstances, and this would mean tracking a group of families over an extended period of time. But even in the absence of such data, the high percentage of Chileans who now have access to schooling, coupled with the country's other healthy social indicators, suggest that there is greater social mobility now and equal opportunity is a reality for a far greater proportion of the populace.

We have endeavored to demonstrate in this chapter that despite a history of unequal income distribution Chile can boast very strong social gains. The poverty rate is being brought down rapidly, consumption (when fiscal policy is factored in) is more evenly spread, and the country ranks high in quality of life indicators.

NOTES

The authors are indebted to Héctor Casanueva, Osvaldo Larrañaga, Andrés Sanfuentes, Arístides Torche, and Rodrigo Vergara for their helpful comments. We are grateful as well to Carmen Celedón and Mario Marcel, who contributed to our understanding of the issues discussed in this chapter. Any remaining errors are our sole responsibility.

1. Encuesta CASEN (Encuesta de Caracterización Socioeconómica Nacional) is a household survey carried out every two years.

2. For a discussion of international comparisons, see Deininger and Squire 1995a.

3. Since x percent of the poorest households takes in more people than x percent of the poorest population, the income of that fraction of households is higher than that of the same fraction of individuals.

4. This is where the distribution of social expenditure should be more equitable than the distribution of autonomous income.

5. Reasons for the heavy cyclical element in the 1992 and 1994 figures, such that elimination of that component should make for an intermediate distribution, are discussed in the following subsection.

6. Our findings tally with those of Agosín (1995), according to whose simulations in a "best" redistribution scenario the share of total income claimed by the poorest 30 percent would rise from 6.2 percent in 1994 to 8.8 percent in 2010.

7. See, for example, Blejer and Guerrero 1990, Cardoso, Paes de Barros, and Urani 1995, and De Gregorio 1995.

8. See especially Blank and Card 1993.

9. Because CASEN does not allow for the tracking of named individuals, it is impossible to know whether the persons who comprised the bottom decile in 1992 were the same as in 1994. More to the point, there is no way of knowing whether the newly unemployed were already in the bottom decile in 1992. Hence, the initially plausible hypothesis that increases in unemployment rates hit the poorest the hardest is ultimately untenable.

10. In any event, some people would need to be rising out of this group in order to keep the proportion constant.

11. Note that the unemployment effect is more pronounced for the B-T ratio; there is less of a change in the MID and the Gini since the unemployment effect is especially strong in the bottom quintile.

12. This is defined as the number of persons who rely on an income earner for sustenance.

13. An extreme position, for instance, would be to advocate that spending be 100 percent targeted to the bottom quintile, but this would be a rather simplistic approach to the question of targeting. For one thing, targeting has a cost: the target group has first to be identified. Handing out free milk at subway exits would be a very inexpensive but hopelessly mistargeted move. Moving to the other extreme, it would be far better to give milk to people who meet certain criteria as to income, nutritional status, age, and so on, but such a scheme, while finely targeted, would be very expensive to operate. While the trend is toward targeting, there is a logical limit to what targeting can do. Furthermore, overtargeting can strongly affect the economic behavior of those not directly targeted.

14. For a detailed account of calculations of the impact of 1992 social spending, see MIDEPLAN 1990.

15. These figures must be analyzed with caution and allowing for a wide margin of error. Apart from the methodology problems typical of income distribution surveys, there can be problems in imputing social spending (see MIDEPLAN 1990 for a description of the methodology used).

16. According to preliminary MIDEPLAN estimates, the targeting of social expenditure improved from 1992 to 1994, as a result of which the poorest quintile received more than the 6.3 percent of total income presented in table 8.4.

17. The poverty rate is the percentage of the population whose per capita income falls below a "poverty line," typically calculated from a basic food basket that can satisfy nutritional needs and takes account of consumer habits. Chile has adopted the term *indigence line* to denote the cost of the basic food basket and defines as *indigent* members of households with a per capita income below that line. The poverty line is double the indigence line for urban areas and 75 percent higher for rural areas. In 1994, the estimated monthly cost of the basic basket of staples was Ch$15,050 for urban and Ch$11,597 for rural dwellers.

18. Contreras (1995) tracked poverty in Chile from 1987 to 1992 using regional baskets of staples and taking into account differences in household

composition. Irarrázaval (1994) made some methodology corrections for calculating "own" income and ascertained the cost of certain food transfers to households to help satisfy basic dietary needs.

19. See Larrañaga 1994, Contreras 1995, and MIDEPLAN 1995a.

20. As will be noted later in this chapter, cross-country comparisons of fractions of poor households require caution, since each country bases its calculations on its own poverty cutoff line. It thus should not surprise us that some of the countries included in the table report less than 20 percent of households living in poverty.

21. Poverty rates are calculated adjusting the exchange rate of each pair by purchasing power parity to take account of cost of living differences.

22. We opted for this source because our calculations could be done with disaggregated data. Since poverty diminished between 1992 and 1994, 1994 calculations for Chile could be expected to yield a more positive picture.

23. Contradictory as it may seem, the indigence level can decrease despite a drop in average income in the bottom decile. Even if average per capita income falls, a more or less even distribution within that decile can lower poverty.

24. This method has been used by Larrañaga (1994). It assumes 1.5 percent population growth.

25. According to Pardo et al. (1992), who opted for a different methodology, economic growth (and notably labor market behavior) played a prominent role in easing poverty between 1987 and 1990.

26. Hence, $g = g_A + g_E$.

27. For an in-depth discussion of determinants of economic growth, see Barro and Sala-i-Martin 1995.

28. See, for example, Larraín and Vergara 1992, Persson and Tabellini 1994, Galor and Zeira 1993, Bertola 1993, and Alesina and Rodrik 1994. Bénabou 1996 and Perotti 1996 offer recent reviews of the literature.

29. Features of this approach are an initial definition of a set of basic needs, followed by a selection of variables or benchmarks to gauge how fully these needs are satisfied, and finally a determination of a minimum value for each indicator. Households for whom one or more basic needs are not being met are classed as poor. Work with this approach has been done by Teitelboim (1992).

30. See, for example, De Gregorio 1996, Barro 1991, King and Levine 1993, and Corbo and Rojas 1992.

REFERENCES

Agosín, M. 1995. Proyecciones y escenarios de largo plazo para la economía chilena. In *Sustentabilidad ambiental del crecimiento económico chileno.* Santiago: Andros Productora Gráfica.

Alesina, A., and D. Rodrik. 1994. Distributive Politics and Economic Growth. *Quarterly Journal of Economics* 109:465–90.

Barro, R. 1991. Economic Growth in a Cross Section of Countries. *Quarterly Journal of Economics* 104:407–33.

Barro, R., and X. Sala-i-Martin. 1995. *Economic Growth.* New York: McGraw-Hill.

Bénabou, R. 1996. Inequality and Growth. *NBER Macroeconomics Annual 1996.* Cambridge: MIT Press.

Bertola, G. 1993. Factor Shares and Savings in Endogenous Growth. *American Economic Review* 83:1184–98.

Beyer, H. 1995. Logros en pobreza, ¿frustración en la igualdad? *Estudios Públicos* 60:15–33.

Blank, R., and D. Card. 1993. Poverty, Income Distribution and Growth: Are They Still Connected? *Brookings Papers on Economic Activity* 2:286–339.

Blejer, M., and I. Guerrero. 1990. The Impact of Macroeconomic Policies on Income Distribution: An Empirical Study of the Philippines. *Review of Economics and Statistics* 72:414–23.

Cardoso, E., R. Paes de Barros, and A. Urani. 1995. Macroeconomic Instability and Income Distribution in Brazil. In R. Dornbusch and S. Edwards, eds., *Reform, Recovery, and Growth: Latin America and the Middle East.* Chicago: University of Chicago Press.

CEPAL. 1995. *Situación de la pobreza en Chile.* 1994 CASEN survey. Mimeo.

Chen, S., G. Datt, and M. Ravallion. 1994. Is Poverty Increasing in the Developing World? *Review of Income and Wealth* 4:359–75.

Contreras, D. 1995. Poverty Measures, Robustness of the Poverty Profiles, Welfare, and Targeting: Evidence from Chile. UCLA. Mimeo.

Corbo, V., and P. Rojas. 1992. Crecimiento económico de América Latina. *Cuadernos de Economía* 87:265–81.

De Gregorio, J. 1995. Comments. In R. Dornbusch and S. Edwards, eds., *Reform, Recovery, and Growth: Latin America and the Middle East.* Chicago: University of Chicago Press.

———. 1996. Borrowing Constraints, Education, and Growth. *Journal of Monetary Economics* 37:41–47.

Deininger, K., and L. Squire. 1995a. Measuring Income Distribution: A New Data-Base. World Bank. Mimeo.

———. 1995b. Inequality and Growth: Results from a New Data Set. World Bank. Mimeo.

Galor, O., and J. Zeira. 1993. Income Distribution and Macroeconomics. *Review of Economic Studies* 60:35–52.

Irarrázaval, I. 1994. Pobreza: la gran tarea. In F. Larraín, ed., *Chile hacia el 2000.* Santiago: Centro de Estudios Públicos.

King, R., and R. Levine. 1993. Finance and Growth: Schumpeter Might Be Right. *Quarterly Journal of Economics* 108:717–37.

Kuznetz, S. 1955. Economic Growth and Income Inequality. *American Economic Review* 45:1–28.

Larraín, F., and R. Vergara. 1992. Distribución del ingreso, inversión, y crecimiento. *Cuadernos de Economía* 87:207–28.

Larrañaga, O. 1994. Pobreza, crecimiento, y desigualdad: Chile, 1987–1992. *Revista de Análisis Económico* 2:69–92.

Marcel, M., and A. Solimano. 1994. The Distribution of Income and Economic Adjustment. In B. Bosworth, R. Dornbusch, and R. Labán, eds., *The*

Chilean Economy: Policy Lessons and Challenges. Washington, DC: Brookings Institution.

MIDEPLAN (Chilean Planning Ministry). 1990. *Programas sociales: su impacto en los hogares chilenos: CASEN 1990.* Santiago: Alfabeta Editores.

———. 1994. *Integración al desarrollo. Balance de la política social, 1990–1993.* Santiago: Alfabeta Editores.

———. 1995a. *Chile: Incidencia e intensidad de la pobreza, 1992–1994.* Santiago: Serie Documentos Económicos.

———. 1995b. Evolución de los ingresos de los hogares según Encuesta CASEN, 1992–1994. Mimeo.

Ministry of Finance, Chile. 1995. *Estadísticas de las Finanzes Públicas 1990–94.* Santiago: Ministerio de Haciende.

Pardo, L., F. Balmaceda, and I. Irarrázaval. 1992. Pobreza, crecimiento y políticas sociales. In *Comentarios sobre la situación económica, 1992.* Santiago: Economics Department, University of Chile.

Perotti, R. 1996. Growth, Income Distribution, and Democracy: What the Data Say. *Journal of Economic Growth* 1:149–211.

Persson, T., and G. Tabellini. 1994. Is Inequality Harmful for Growth? Theory and Evidence. *American Economic Review* 81:600–619.

Solon, G. 1992. Intergenerational Mobility in the United States. *American Economic Review* 82:393–408.

Teitelboim, B. 1992. Dimensión y características de la pobreza. In *Población, educación, vivienda, salud, empleo, y pobreza.* Santiago: Alfabeta Impresores.

UNDP. 1995. *Human Development Report.* New York: Oxford University Press.

World Bank. 1990. *World Development Report.* Washington, DC: World Bank.

———. 1995. *World Development Report.* Washington, DC: World Bank.

Zimmerman, D. J. 1992. Regression toward Mediocrity in Economic Stature. *American Economic Review* 82:409–29.

CHAPTER 9

Economic Growth, Fiscal Policy, and Social Impact in Chile

José Pablo Arellano

This chapter takes up three basic issues relating to fiscal policy and its contribution to the attainment of greater social equity and economic growth in Chile. The primary focus is on the years 1990–96, which is the period during which it has been my privilege to participate in the setting of Chilean fiscal policy. Specifically, I should like to touch on three main aspects: first, the resources available for fiscal policy measures; second, the efforts made to lessen the impact of fiscal policy on the poor; and third, identification of future challenges and opportunities in the areas of social equity and fiscal policy.

Resources and Poverty Targeting

Regarding availability of fiscal resources, the new democratic government taking office in 1990 did so on a platform that included making a clean break with the previous philosophy concerning the amount of public funds dedicated to fiscal policy. We made a clear-cut decision at that time to reverse the trend toward lower taxes that had prevailed in the years leading up to this period in order to pay for an increase in social benefits. The dotted line in figure 9.1 represents per capita income, and the straight line indicates the ratio of tax proceeds to GDP (i.e., the tax burden), showing the drop in the latter in the years prior to 1989–90. With the fiscal reforms carried out in 1990, we were able to bring the tax burden to the levels that we have today, namely, 17 percent of GDP. This was the counterpart on the revenues side that was needed to finance the social spending I am about to describe while maintaining and consolidating the fiscal position.

I should like at this point to refer to table 9.1, which shows the fiscal position in recent years. Note that government savings ("current surplus") reached some 5.5 percent of GDP in 1995, while the overall fiscal

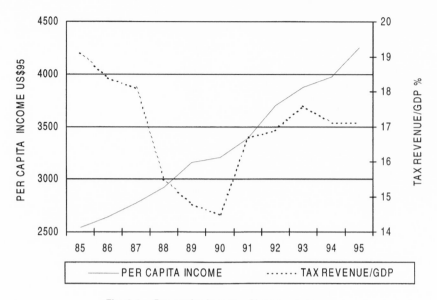

Fig. 9.1. Per capita income: Net tax revenues

surplus has been around 2 percent of GDP. The fiscal position has clearly improved since 1990. There is another line as well, which is barely visible after the overall balance in table 9.1. It represents deposits in the copper stabilization fund. This is a device for stabilizing the price of copper, which is added to previous balances and which—with the price of copper up last year—reached 1 percent of GDP. The effect of this solid fiscal performance has been to lower foreign debt from more than U.S.$7 billion at the end of the 1980s to U.S.$4.8 billion in 1995.

At the same time, there has been a major increase in social spending. The last line in table 9.1 is for social expenditure. It indicates that the amount allocated for this sector has risen at an effective annual rate of 8.5 percent between 1991 and 1995. This contrasts with what was happening in prior years, as in 1989–90 when social spending actually declined. In other words, there was a major change in direction beginning in 1990, with greater resources being directed into social programs while at the same time a solid fiscal position was maintained.

I emphasize the importance of our sound fiscal position because I believe that this, together with other variables, has enabled us to create a kind of virtuous circle in which increased national savings have meant greater investment, leading to accelerated economic growth, which in turn has yielded resources that can be allocated to social programs. Two

TABLE 9.1. Chile: Central Government, 1987–95 (percentage of GDP)

	1987	1988	1989	1990	1991	1992	1993	1994	1995
Current revenues	25.2	22.3	21.2	20.5	22.3	22.4	22.6	21.9	22.3
Tax revenues	18.1	15.5	14.8	14.5	16.7	16.9	17.6	17.1	17.1
Current expenditures	22.2	20.0	18.2	18.1	18.6	17.5	17.7	17.2	16.9
Current Surplus	3.0	2.3	3.0	2.5	3.7	4.9	4.8	4.8	5.5
Capital expenditures	3.3	3.9	3.6	2.9	3.2	3.7	3.7	3.9	3.6
Overall Surplus	1.9	1.0	1.4	0.8	1.5	2.2	1.9	1.7	2.6
Deposits in the Copper Stabilization Fund	0.5	3.0	3.7	2.3	0.7	0.3	−0.2	0.2	1.1
External public debt (millions of U.S.$)	7,103	7,033	6,747	6,743	6,201	6,295	5,756	5,834	4,849
Social Expenditures (annual % change)		3.3	−1.0	−0.9	9.3	10.6	9.6	6.1	7.1

Source: Budget Office, Ministry of Finance.

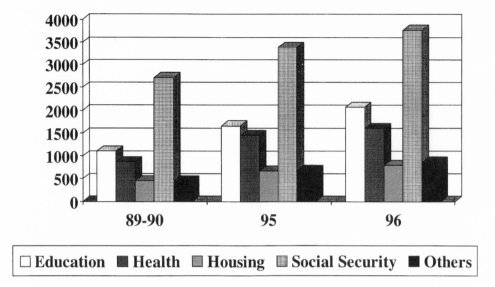

Fig. 9.2.   **Increase in social resources (millions of U.S.$)**

figures, in particular, demonstrate the increased availability of resources for social programs during this period: social spending rose by 50 percent in real terms over the period 1990–95, and 85 percent of the total rise in government spending over this same period was channeled into social programs.

As figure 9.2 demonstrates, large increases have been posted in all areas of social expenditure. Spending on education (first bar) has risen significantly, particularly in 1995–96; health has achieved the greatest increase, although growth has slowed recently; and, while housing (third bar) and social security or pensions (fourth bar) are the most in need of additional resources, they are also the sectors in which growth has been slowest. I should like to present an example or two in each area of the government's social agenda to illustrate the effort being made to enhance the distributive impact of the nation's fiscal policy.

Beginning with education, a sector analyzed in greater detail in the chapters by Sergio Molina and Eduardo Aninat, it should be noted first of all that 61 percent of the investment in education goes to the poorest 40 percent of the population and that 35 percent of total resources goes to the poorest 20 percent. There are several progressive programs directed at improving the quality of education in the poorest schools. One example is the 900 schools program (although there are now close to 1,500 schools involved), which has so far raised average scores on achievement tests at participating institutions to more than the national average.

Another example is the increase in the per capita educational grant provided by the government. Under Chile's educational system, schools receive a grant for each student in attendance, and these grants follow individual students wherever they go. The increase in this capitation grant has been especially important in rural areas, where the rise in grant levels per student has been proportionately greater than in nonrural areas.

Another hotly debated topic has been the introduction of a shared funding system for education whereby parents who are able to do so may help finance the schools that their children attend, thereby reducing the amount of the state's subsidy to such institutions. Parents able to contribute to school financing are given special payment vouchers for this purpose. This system has been developed for distributive purposes and for increasing the resources available for education, and we believe that it represents a promising reform. A special program to improve the quality of education, which is described in the chapter by Sergio Molina, involves increasing the resources allotted for school nutrition programs and lengthening the school day. As well, certain experimental programs to strengthen schools attended by children with learning disabilities have been implemented in the last two years.

The budget allocation for higher education has also gone up, although the rise has been less than that for the system as a whole. Higher education received 18 percent of the state's total education budget in 1991, whereas this figure dropped to 14 percent in 1995. Most of the increase in actual spending on this sector went to scholarships and student loans.

If we compare changes in per capita income (the solid line in figure 9.3) with changes in the capitation grant (vouchers) for students in basic or primary education, we see that after the period leading up to 1990, in which the amount per student remained constant or even declined, there has been a steady and systematic rise in the real value of student vouchers every year during the 1990s.

Figure 9.4 shows the number of school lunches and breakfasts provided, and here again the line either slopes downward or remains flat up to the year 1989, after which it climbs steadily throughout the 1990s. In addition, this is a highly targeted program aimed at children most in need of help.

The health sector is another area in which the state's resources are directed primarily toward the poor: 83 percent of total resources goes to the poorest 40 percent and 50 percent to the poorest 20 percent of the population. The people served by the public health sector are from the

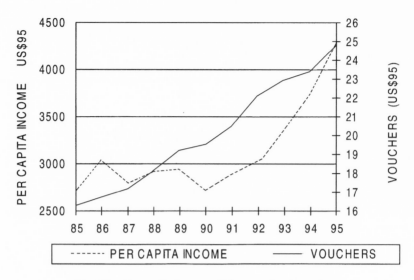

Fig. 9.3.   Per capita income: Primary school vouchers

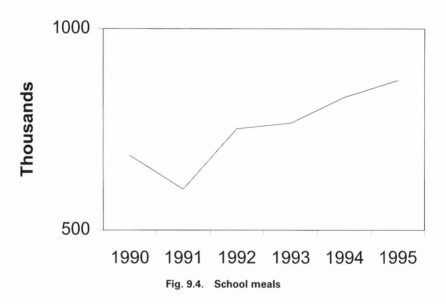

Fig. 9.4.   School meals

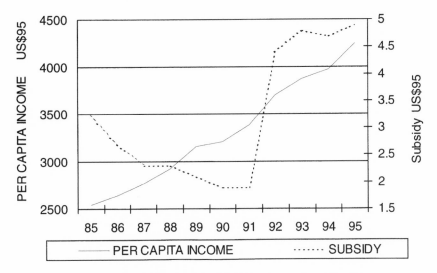

Fig. 9.5. Per capita income: Subsidies for medical attention

poorest segments of Chilean society. Two aspects of the health sector can be mentioned in passing. The first is the priority being given to primary care in the form of additional funding for this sector and the changeover to a system of per capita payments for individuals registering with the primary care services. The second is the fact that those who opt for the private health care system also receive a capitation subsidy from the state, the amount of which has been rising (again, compared to per capita income), as is shown in figure 9.5.

In the area of housing, I should like to mention two or three items. First, new housing programs from 1990 on have been designed with the needs of the poorest sectors in mind. Two of these come immediately to mind. One is the basic housing program, which follows the traditional approach of providing families with serviced lots and technical assistance so that they can gradually enlarge their housing units to meet growing needs. A second important program provides subsidies to rural families for the construction of basic housing units along these same lines. The second item with respect to housing is that subsidies for middle-income families have been reduced. Chile has a low-cost housing system that grants recipients an initial lump sum to purchase housing, the amount of which varies according to the value of the housing unit and the family's income level. The amount of this subsidy has been dropping for middle-income families so that the resultant savings can be redirected toward the worst off among low-income groups. A third important aspect is the

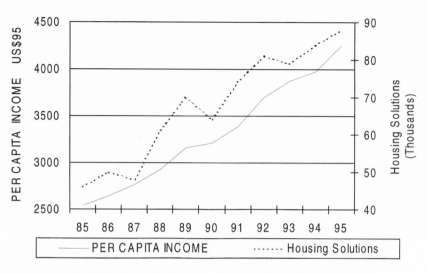

Fig. 9.6.   Per capita income: Number of housing solutions

growing effort in recent years to provide basic services for the poor in urban areas by targeting resources so that they reach the poorest families living in cramped housing where the need for social infrastructure is greatest.

In the last few years it has been possible to increase housing construction at a rate faster than population growth, thereby reducing the housing shortage. The dotted line in figure 9.6 shows that the number of housing solutions has increased at a higher rate than per capita income. The middle bar in figure 9.7 represents housing subsidies paid to middle-income groups. Note that this amount has gone down while the resources allocated to housing for low-income groups has risen, almost doubling over the period 1990–95 compared to the second half of the 1980s.

The subsidized water supply is another area where priority is being placed on the targeting of resources. The basic approach in this area has been one of increasing water and sanitation rates (so as to make these utilities self-supporting by bringing their charges into line with costs) while at the same time providing subsidies for the poorest households. Slightly more than 10 percent of households receive this subsidy, the amount of which is based on minimum water consumption and is calculated to enable the utility companies to finance their investments through the contributions of middle-income families.

Finally, there is the matter of user-fee arrangements such as highway concessions (toll roads), which I believe is a very important concept

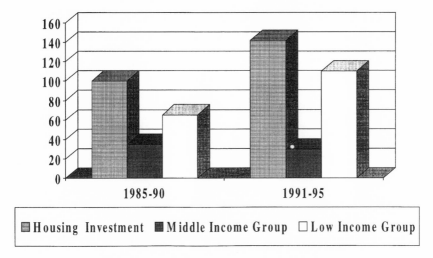

Fig. 9.7. **Participation in housing investment**

from the standpoint of increasing the contribution that the actual users of our infrastructure are expected to make.

In the area of social security and Chile's contributory pension plan, 12 percent of resources go to the poorest 40 percent of recipients. Contributory pension plans are those to which individuals contribute during their working lives so that there is a much closer correlation with the income of recipients. At the same time, there is also a noncontributory or welfare pension program for low-income families and elderly people living in poverty, under which 60 percent of total resources go the poorest 40 percent in this category. Here, the policy has been to give special increases above the rate of inflation in the case of the lowest benefit levels (see figs. 9.8 and 9.9).

Targeting has been sharpened in the field of family allowances as well, with the elimination of payments to high-income groups and the boosting of allowances for those in the lowest categories. Minimum benefit levels for those outside the formal economy, and therefore under the so-called noncontributory or welfare pension program, have also been raised considerably. Benefits paid under the family allowance and combined family benefit plans have been increasing in real terms since 1990, with improved targeting due to the elimination of subsidies for the higher income groups.

I should like to briefly mention several new programs worth noting. First, a number of funds have been created to which the poorest

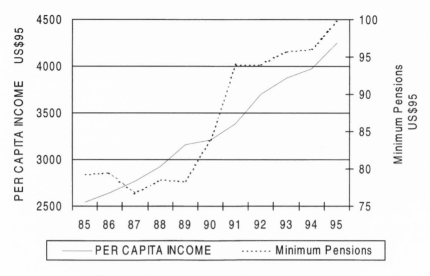

Fig. 9.8.   Per capita income: Minimum pensions

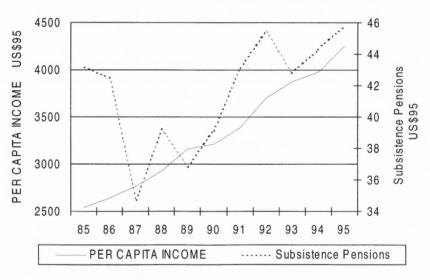

Fig. 9.9.   Per capita income: Subsistence pensions

communities can submit proposals for local construction projects, equipment, and so on. Second, an interesting program aimed at small producers in the informal sector has been developed under which these microentrepreneurs can obtain subsidized loans under a competitive system and with a subsidy of approximately U.S.$70 per transaction. The intention is to put Chile's financial institutions into contact with microentrepreneurs who have achieved increasingly good results. Another successful effort is that of the land titling programs, particularly in rural areas.

A special and very interesting job training program for young people is being carried out with the Inter-American Development Bank (IDB). And, finally, efforts are being made to sharpen the targeting of subsidy programs in irrigation and forestry projects to ensure that the benefits go to low-income producers. New telephone, electrification, and water subsidy programs have been created to assist those living in rural areas. These new programs have garnered a growing share of resources in recent years.

In sum, there has been not only a large increase in the amount of resources allocated to social programs but also a concerted effort to improve targeting so that more of the benefits go to the poorest segments of the population.

Challenges and Opportunities

To end this discussion, I should like to mention a few of the challenges and opportunities in store for those responsible for designing and implementing Chile's future social policies. First is the matter of resources. If the economy grows at an annual rate of 6 percent or more, what is the volume of resources we will have to direct toward low-income groups? Let us assume for a moment that we continue to allocate nearly 14 percent of our output to social programs and that Chile's Congress votes to retain taxes such as the VAT. How much in the way of resources will this leave us to direct toward the poorest 40 percent of our people, more than the 6 percent growth rate, or less? I would suggest that we will see less than a 6 percent rise in the amount of resources directed toward the poorest 40 percent of the population for the simple reason that a good portion of spending on social programs goes into salaries since these sectors have a very large wage component. If the economy grows at a 6 percent rate, wages will rise by at least 4 percent, and this will be as true for health and education as anywhere else in the economy. In addition, we are facing an inevitable rise in pension payouts over the next few years due to population growth. For this

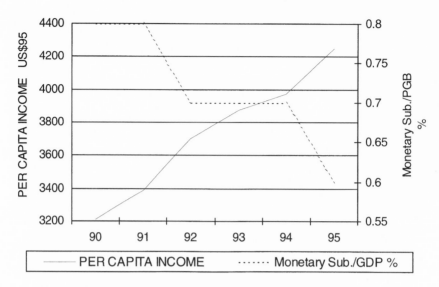

Fig. 9.10.   Per capita income: Monetary subsidies

reason, it is my view that if we can channel all our available resources, after deducting wage hikes and the increase in pensions, we will be left with a figure under our fiscal policy equivalent to, at most, approximately 4.5 percent per year. This will be due to the increase in personal income and the reassignment of the same to headings other than social expenditures or infrastructure. This will total roughly 5 percent of output and includes defense and the more traditional administrative tasks. Consequently, I believe we face a difficult task in terms of the quantity of resources that we can dedicate to social programs — even with a strong rate of economic growth.

The question of where to direct the additional resources generated by economic growth is an important one and in my view comes down to a clear choice between monetary subsidies and pensions, on the one hand, and education and health on the other. As indicated in other chapters, Chile has opted to stress education rather than significantly increasing monetary transfers — as is shown in the figures for the past few years. For, although pensions and transfer payments have seen extraordinary growth in this period, the main effort in Chile's social spending has been directed to education and health. Moreover, we plan to stay the course.

In recent years, growth in transfer payments has not kept pace with output (see fig. 9.10). The dotted line shows monetary transfers as a percentage of output, and, while these have risen in real terms, their rate of growth has not matched that of economic output.

As stated previously, education will be the main focus of Chile's social policy over the next few years. Accordingly, the surveys to determine income distribution are unlikely to change much during that period, despite the very considerable effort being made to improve social programs. This is so because these surveys produce statistics on primary income distribution, whereas monetary subsidies are not going to increase in the same proportion as per capita income.

Finally, it is important to remember that in the stage of economic development Chile is now entering new social welfare programs will differ from the traditional approach, placing greater emphasis on quality of life and the provision of access to quasi-public goods — another category not recorded among monetary subsidies. It is our hope that these new programs will raise the standard of living among Chileans, enabling us to make growth and social equity a reality.

CHAPTER 10

Educational Reform in Chile

Sergio Molina

During the administration of Eduardo Frei Montalva in the 1960s, Chile undertook a far-reaching reform effort designed to give all Chilean children access to education. The major issue at the time was poor coverage and low enrollment. Over the next 30 years, a determined effort was made to improve the situation, so that today coverage is close to 95 percent for elementary education and 80 percent for secondary education. At the preschool level, we still have a deficit of nearly 27 percent. The main problem is with children under four; coverage in the last year of preschool, when children make the transition to primary school, is satisfactory. Raising coverage in the early years not only carries a high cost but introduces cultural contradictions since there is a marked trend among mothers caring for their children during these years. In short, elementary and secondary school coverage is satisfactory in Chile. However, there is a widespread consensus that quality is inadequate and distribution unequal.

The current distribution of school enrollment is 8 percent at paid private schools, 32 percent at state-subsidized (free) private schools, and 60 percent at municipally run schools that belonged to the Ministry of Education prior to 1981. Although academic performance is lowest at municipal schools, no direct comparisons can be made since these schools have the highest proportion of students from low-income families. In addition, insufficient funding was transferred by the state, and not enough technical assistance was given to municipal staff.

In the wake of the 1982 crisis, state contributions to municipalities were cut substantially. As a result, when the first democratic government came into power in 1990, teachers were extraordinarily poorly paid, municipalities lacked funding to maintain the schools properly, and the quality of education was steadily declining. Thus, our task is to improve the quality of education and make it more equitable.

Changes in Quality

Educational Content

One of the major changes is in what is being taught. Chile had not altered its basic objectives or the mandatory content of education in 25 years. Modifications for elementary education were approved in 1996. Implementation for all eight years of elementary school will be completed by 2001.

The thrust of the change is to update the curriculum in order to adapt it to new needs in today's environment. Educational establishments will be able to devise programs that take advantage of their areas of specialization while including the mandatory components that lend consistency to the system. This will enable each establishment to initiate a participatory process within the school community, tailoring the curriculum to unique geographical features and the interests of the community and thus diversifying the school system overall.

The secondary school curriculum is being updated by our country's best experts in conjunction with highly qualified foreign consultants. A proposal will be prepared in 1996 for consideration by the major players in the educational system, and their observations will be taken into account prior to official approval in 1997. The new curriculum is expected to be completed by 2001. At that point, the basic objectives and mandatory content of Chilean education will have been completely overhauled and updated to equip children and young people to function successfully in the "knowledge era."

Methods

It is a fact that teaching methods in Chile are outdated and ill suited to a world of dizzying change. Children and young people need to "learn how to learn," to take part in a process of discovering knowledge working in groups rather than as individuals. This must be done by making the best use of the resources available and bringing schools into the real world.

Learning takes precedence over teaching. The frontal classroom approach quickly becomes routine and monotonous for both teachers and students. Learning can be fun, can awaken the students' creativity and accustom them to solving problems, giving them the versatility they will need to deal intelligently with the changing situations they will encounter throughout their lives. This is a goal we are pursuing by training our teachers.

Resources

Curriculum changes and new teaching methods call for updated text-books and teaching materials. The former is a consequence of the change in educational content, the latter of new ways of teaching. New textbooks are being written with the inclusion of material that will foster a group approach to problem solving. Alongside these necessary modifications are three highly innovative programs:

First, well-equipped libraries will be provided to all secondary schools. This is crucial to promote research and reading. On a somewhat less sophisticated level, the provision of classroom libraries to all elementary schools will be completed in 1997. This program is designed to stimulate good reading habits in children from their earliest years.

A second innovation is the inclusion of information technology in the school system. The idea is not to teach computer classes but to have children use computers as a modern tool for learning.

Agreement has been reached with 26 universities to provide technical assistance to all the schools in the system. This will promote communication among them and with the universities. Internet connections will immediately open a window onto the world for all secondary students and 50 percent of elementary students by 2000. This will bring about a genuine renewal within schools for both teachers and students.

Finally, educational television will be introduced in 1996 to enable teachers to use the best programs being produced worldwide. National experts are also developing components for delivery to the schools. This is a very important tool for modernizing education.

Class Hours

Changes in the curriculum, teaching methods, and resources have made it necessary to extend the school day. A steady rise in coverage without a matching expansion in infrastructure has led to schools being used in two and even three shifts per day. This has two undesirable consequences. First, class hours are insufficient, and, second, resources (libraries, information technology, educational television) cannot be used efficiently in a school day subject to tight time constraints. Also, teachers do not have enough time available for preparation or for meeting with students, parents, and guardians.

The government intends to have all schools operating on a single shift by 2002. This will mean making a substantial investment in infrastructure and increasing public subsidies to fund the extended school day. The benefits of taking this step are clear. It will improve the quality of education, promote better academic performance, enable teachers to work at a single school, and provide greater protection for children when both parents work. Finally, it is important that teachers and students identify with their school and look after its interests.

The "full school day" that has started to be implemented is the culmination of a reform of the Chilean educational system that is broader and more far-reaching than any other in this century. The state subsidy obtainable in exchange for an extended school day will naturally be subject to requirements such as having adequate infrastructure available, coming up with a program that indicates how additional hours are to be used, and having the necessary teaching and administrative staff to ensure that the program will be carried out.

Quality High Schools

Finally, it has been suggested that recognition be given to high schools meeting certain requirements indicative of quality or innovation to serve as models for others. These schools are to meet unique standards of administration, with greater participation by members of their communities and more autonomous decision-making authority. The teaching staff is also to meet special training requirements, adequate infrastructure must be available to accommodate students in a single shift, tuition must be free of charge, and low-income students must be welcomed to prevent an elitist slant. Schools meeting these requirements will receive special state support. A geographical and social balance will be sought to ensure that the positive effects are passed on throughout the country to all social groups, serving as an incentive and an example for all the country's high schools.

Equity

Widespread changes in the quality of education generally bring greater benefits to the less affluent in society. Accordingly, the widespread improvement in quality now under way in Chile is engendering a marked improvement in the system's equity as well. Here I would like to refer to some of the programs being targeted to the groups that lag furthest behind.

Slow-Growth Schools

Since this program was originally designed to help 900 schools, it is known as "P–900." Today some 10 percent of elementary schools are targeted for the training of monitors (young people) from the community, grants of assistance from the Ministry of Education, the provision of adequate and efficient teaching materials, and so on. Since this program has been under way since 1990, it is now possible to gauge its results. I would simply point out that students at these schools have performed better than the national average. Programs such as these enable public resources to be targeted directly to poorer groups.

Improving Rural Education

Rural education undeniably lags behind in almost all countries. In Chile, we have developed a special program to supply new textbooks and teaching materials, provide technical assistance and additional state subsidies, and set up microcenters as meeting places where rural teachers — especially those in more remote areas — can share their experiences and receive technical assistance. Although rural students account for just 15 percent of the total in Chile, we still have far to go before the educational opportunities open to rural students match those available in the cities.

Special Academic Help

A program was implemented in 1996 to give special help to students lagging behind and thereby prevent grade repetition and dropping out. This program is potentially very important, since repetition, in addition to its high cost, affects mainly the poorest groups and often causes young people to drop out of school.

Welfare Policies

Chile has had a school nutrition program (PAE) in place for many years. Targeted especially to poor children, it has yielded magnificent results, both in terms of improving nutrition and in promoting better school attendance, retention, and performance. The nutrition program serves about 900,000 children, almost all of them from families in the first and second income quintiles.

There is also a health care program for poor students up to the fifth grade. This program has played a vital role in the timely diagnosis and treatment of illnesses that can affect students' health and their ability to learn. In the limited time available to me, I will mention those programs that are most important and have had the greatest impact on the educational process.

Teacher Training

The reform program accords the highest importance to training teachers, since it is in the classroom — between teachers and students — that the results of the reform will be demonstrated. I will list the main sections included in the program.

Initial Training

A system of agreements with teachers' colleges and faculties of education has been implemented to improve teacher education, purchase modern teaching materials, provide proper libraries, improve infrastructure in relation to projects that will boost academic quality, and so on. Special scholarships are envisaged for qualified students who wish to study teaching in order to raise the quality of applicants and consequently of future teachers.

Upgrading

The program calls for basic upgrading — returning to a university for a limited time — for 20 percent of all teachers in the next three years. A five million dollar fund was created in 1996 to provide fellowships to finance short periods of study and longer postgraduate studies abroad. Finally, the existing programs providing upgrading for teachers in service will remain in effect. These are linked primarily to innovative programs being implemented by the ministry and cover about 50 percent of teachers each year.

Working Conditions

Generally speaking, the physical working conditions of teaching professionals are inadequate. Many schools lack meeting rooms and cafeterias, and sanitary conditions are substandard. A considerable effort has been made in this area because improving conditions in the workplace not only improves teacher performance but enhances teacher dignity.

The second issue is pay. Despite major efforts by two democratic administrations from 1990 to 1996 — which have resulted in an average 80 percent increase in real terms — pay levels are still lower than those of other professionals in public service. Teachers' pay levels must be raised gradually to match the value attached to this work. It is crucial that teachers welcome the reform under way in a spirit of enthusiasm and leadership. If we can set the stage to improve initial teacher training, retrain those now in service, improve working conditions, and raise pay levels, we will have laid the groundwork for effective and lasting reform.

Administration

I would like to say a few words on this issue, which is vital but has not met with as much success as other areas of reform. The most important links in the administrative chain have not yet been adapted to decentralization. I refer to the Ministry of Education, the municipalities, and the schools themselves. The ministry is effectively fulfilling a support function through projects intended to improve the quality and equity of education (MECE) and specific projects targeted to groups lagging behind. However, its administrative structure continues to be centralized and cumbersome, and a long tradition of controls have made for sluggish progress toward the new function of supporting municipalities and schools. Modernization of the Ministry of Education is under way, but the pace must be accelerated if it is to meet the demands of reform.

The municipalities (mayor's offices), which run elementary and high schools, have undergone a protracted and arduous process of adapting to the critical task of administering the public schools, which account for 60 percent of the Chilean school system. I have already pointed out that insufficient training was provided for teaching staff and inadequate resources were transferred when educational administration was passed on to the municipalities in 1981. The democratic administrations in power since 1990 have made a significant effort, in terms of finances and staff training, to improve municipal administration.

Much remains to be done in the area of the schools themselves. They lack financial and administrative autonomy, do not have juridical status, and cannot make independent decisions, even on minor matters. Legislation has been amended since 1995 so that the municipalities can delegate some or all of their powers to school principals.

Finally, I would point to an important program that was initiated (on a pilot basis) in 1996. I refer to the requirement that all Chilean municipalities must devise an annual plan for the development of municipal education (PADEM). This plan is prepared on the basis of the proposals drawn up by each school community for the following year. The Department of Education in each municipality prepares a consolidated plan, which must be approved by the Municipal Council. At year's end, the plan for the next year is prepared and the results for the previous year are published. This is an important means of incorporating communities into the formulation and dissemination of the results of municipal school administration. Finally, the government has launched a gradual process of decentralization to promote greater participation by parents and guardians (families) in the education of their children.

This brief overview of the educational reform now under way in Chile shows that it can be expected to make an important contribution to meeting the major challenges of the coming century in terms of development potential, overcoming poverty, achieving a more equitable distribution of economic gains, and building a more democratic and caring society.

CHAPTER 11

The Labor Market, Growth, and Equity in Chile

Jorge Arrate

First, I have to admit that I did in fact graduate from Harvard, but that was in the 1960s, which was an extremely interesting decade in the United States and the rest of the world for a number of reasons. In my two years as minister of labor, after having served as minister of education in President Aylwin's government, I have learned that debating labor issues from a one-sided point of view is very risky. Both in Parliament and in public and academic discussions, we often find views that consider the world of work and labor policies to be core factors in a country's productive development. On other occasions, basic labor policies are seen from the standpoint of social equity. Our labor policy attempts to balance these different dimensions, which are not limited to the two views I have mentioned. A third aspect is often omitted — that of humanizing and dignifying work — which was probably more popular in the 1960s than it is today.

I would like to pause here to share a private thought. Just a few days ago, we held a very important meeting of the Productive Development Forum. This is a tripartite forum where labor and business organizations and other civil institutions meet with government officials to discuss productive and social development. At the meeting, our minister of finance, Eduardo Aninat, spoke for an hour and a half on the topic of happiness. This is something we need to consider in our thinking on the future of income distribution. I am quite optimistic that in a country where the minister of finance can spend 90 minutes in a seminar talking about happiness, income distribution can only improve. I will divide my presentation into three parts. In the first, I will make some general comments on the subject of labor. Then I will move on to a brief description of the underpinnings of our system of labor relations. I will end with a discussion of policy. What I have to say is not free from controversy, and I will try to at least mention opposing views as I go along, for the sake of fairness.

Primary Comments

We cannot talk about labor policies today without considering the dizzying changes that have swept our world—changes that have had an extraordinary impact on labor, how it is defined, and how it is organized. The strongest aftershock of these changes is a rising tide of uncertainty. Institutions have become universalized, and the market, democracy, and globalization all involve a very strong element of incertitude. Centrally planned economies, though not very efficient, are more predictable than the market. A dictatorship is less uncertain than a democracy, where government authorities change periodically according to a set formula. An inward-looking economy is more manageable and predictable than one that is open to international trade. Work has always been and continues to be an area where human beings are able to realize their potential. Our days are taken up with family, school, and work. It is difficult to imagine how someone can be happy—whatever we mean by happiness—if he or she is unhappy at work.

Today, work is recognized as a key factor in economic growth. This is because present and future growth is seen as predicated on and spurred by knowledge, and workers are recognized as the carriers of that knowledge. Also, growth has been and continues to be driven by the expansion of trade, which raises the question of relations between the world of work and the conditions required to expand free trade. This is on the agenda of all international forums, including the World Trade Organization (WTO) and the International Labor Organization (ILO). Another point I would like to underscore is that work, more than most other areas of human endeavor in our social existence, sits astride two institutions that have taken hold everywhere in the world—the market and democracy. But these two institutions, in my opinion, are not naturally compatible and can only become so by dint of painstaking social effort. Their foundations are radically antithetical. The market is grounded in the ability to recognize and attach a value to differences, and this is the great virtue of the market system for allocating resources. Democracy, on the other hand, is based on an absolutely artificial assumption. It is an invention of our culture and one of the great achievements of human history—the affirmation that we are all equal, when in fact we are all different. So these two institutions must be reconciled and brought together in a process that does not come about automatically or naturally but must be invented and constructed. This is particularly true in the world of labor. We try to keep all these considerations in mind when designing our policies. We are willing to make tradeoffs to come up with a multidimensional policy whereby — given conditions currently prevailing in Chile — work can be a factor in productive development, can be dealt with in public policy with a sense of social equity, and can contribute to the humanization of our society.

Foundations of the Chilean Labor System

The Chilean labor system has been built on the accretion, over many years, of elements drawn from the oldest tradition of social rights, as reflected in the conventions of the ILO and world experience. But its foundations also mirror specific developments in our country over the last quarter century, elements that have taken a central place in our labor policy. I will mention the five main ones.

First, we have set the boundaries of action by each of the three stakeholders (employers, employees, and government), including a definition of the role of government in labor relations. The cornerstone of our policy is a government that does not intervene in specific labor relations issues within companies. The government guides, regulates, and supervises while establishing tripartite bodies to define overall policies and agreements among the social players. As the counterpart to this first element, the second bears on the definition of companies as a productive union of employers, employees, and the means of production — the basic forum where labor relations are defined and unfold. Based on these two factors, our labor model can be considered a decentralized system of labor relations within a universal classification. A third key element in our policy is the recognition that employers have a broad and entrenched right to manage their companies. At the same time, we validate fully the freedom to organize, whereby workers are allowed to form unions. The fifth factor is recognition of the fundamental attribute of labor organizations, which is the right to collective bargaining, to sit down at the table and participate in civic dialogue and to discuss wages and working conditions.

These are the theoretical and institutional underpinnings of our system of labor relations. They are not in dispute, and we never have and never will attempt to change them. In practice, of course, each is subject to its own vicissitudes. In some areas more than others, this raises problems both in our understanding of them as tenets of the system and in terms of the consequences of their application. In sum, the government's labor policy focuses on the three points I have mentioned: productive development, social equity, and humanization.

Productive Development

On the question of productive development, I would like to examine in some detail three areas that are closely related: balanced labor relations, mobility in the job market, and flexibility.

Balanced Labor Relations

First, we have tried to focus on productivity in a setting of balanced, comparable, and equitable labor relations. In addition to full respect for the right to unionize and the achievement of better protection for unions, this also means extending the right to collective bargaining—still not widespread in Chile today—as well as strict compliance with labor laws. I will comment briefly on these issues before moving on to the second point.

The Chilean union movement, like the country itself and each of us individually at certain points in our lives, is experiencing a period of transition. This probably holds true for the labor movement throughout the world, but in our country old traditions have a uniquely powerful hold. Here I would come back to the issue of uncertainty. One example is the concept of job security or ownership. This notion, though less operational today than in the past owing to modern economic conditions, is enshrined in the culture of the labor movement and has led to resistance to the new realities in the labor market, reflecting uncertainty in the face of change. From the government's viewpoint, we are not looking for unions to take up a monopoly position that will skew the operation of the market; we want them to take a forward-looking approach. This means strengthening their ability to cooperate inside companies. In order to do that, they must be able to sit down at the table on an equal basis with employers to talk about the major issues of growth and development. We believe this means extending the right to collective bargaining. I should stress that neither now nor in the future will the government force anyone to unionize or bargain collectively, since we view these as rights that each individual can choose to exercise. However, we would like to see a higher percentage of workers participating in collective bargaining in Chile, particularly in fields where unions do not exist today and where there are no tripartite or bipartite undertakings but only the unilateral and exclusive will of the employer. This one-sided approach is not acceptable in the sphere of the international principles of labor relations. As for enforcing the law, we have a national supervisory system that is quite effective in comparison with that of other countries. It is a professional and responsible service that has achieved very good management indicators and has been given sufficient funds, under the former and current governments, to build up its staff and carry out an ambitious modernization program, which includes computerized information systems and vehicle purchases, to allow it to better carry out its supervisory activities. We have also passed a law reforming the labor courts to facilitate more expeditious and effective enforcement of labor laws.

Mobility in the Labor Market

The second point I would like to stress in the sphere of productive development has to do with achieving adequate mobility in the job market. This can be achieved by promoting three avenues of policy and three different institutions that must work like cogs in a well-oiled machine: the employment information system, the national training system, and the system for the protection of unemployed workers. Under the national employment information system, we are establishing a network of municipal offices to provide job information as a national clearinghouse for jobs. This is bolstered by a strong training and professional development effort, which I would like to focus on briefly.

In Chile, the training system operates on the basis of a public demand subsidy in the form of a tax exemption for up to 1 percent of the payroll invested in training in the preceding year, which employers can recoup when they pay their taxes. The potential volume of funds available for training is equal to approximately 10 percent of public spending on education, which is a large sum. Although just 28 percent of that potential was realized in 1990, today we have topped the 40 percent mark. We are proud of this achievement, even though it means that all the funds available for job training are not yet being used. The situation has led us to amend the law in an attempt to stimulate a system that has so far depended exclusively on employer initiatives, since employers are the ones who decide when, where, and under what conditions training will be offered and who will benefit from it. Therefore, we are encouraging the establishment of employer-employee training committees in companies, with workers and unions taking part, in order to give them a say in training. We have also introduced an incentive for companies that design training activities in conjunction with their employees, which consists of making more public funds available for the purpose. Furthermore, we are creating a national training fund to provide special financing for those not eligible for the corporate tax deduction: the unemployed, female heads of families, young people lacking resources, and sectors undergoing restructuring or needing preferential financing such as small businesses and microenterprises. The purpose of the fund is to provide more access to the training system, since it is currently targeted chiefly to people with jobs. A third avenue of action that is very important is the youth training program, which has been backed for four years by the IDB and which we have extended for a further three years with government funding in view of its positive results.

The third cog in this engine is a new institution we are about to establish. Commonly known as unemployment insurance, the program is in fact designed to protect unemployed workers. It is not an insurance scheme but instead seeks to protect the mobility of workers by cushioning the impact of uncertainty in finding a new job. The system is based on the establishment of individual savings accounts belonging to workers, which are funded by them, their employers, and supplementary government contributions. These accounts are intended to provide them with savings that can be capitalized to tide them over if their contracts are terminated, if they resign, and under other circumstances for a period that is long enough to enable them to find new work. The employment information system, the national training system, and the system for the protection of the unemployed are three mechanisms that should make our labor market work more effectively and minimize the uncertainty and distress associated with job mobility for those who are literally suffering the effects of change.

Labor Flexibility

The third aspect of productive development is flexibility, which I consider to be of the utmost importance. In our country, we have some of the most flexible rules governing dismissal in the world. In this field, we would like to strengthen both internal and external flexibility. Normally, when we speak of flexibility in Chile we think of finding or leaving a job, which is external flexibility. What we would like to do is to strengthen mechanisms for internal flexibility — making labor adjustments inside companies. Our proposal involves a series of standards on internal flexibility agreed upon by unions and employers, which do not exist today in Chilean legislation: establishing monthly rather than daily hours of work, wage reduction agreements in return for job stability, and layoffs for up to six months as an alternative to dismissal in the event that a company is hit by an economic crisis. These proposals have led to more heated debate with the unions than our proposals on protection of the right to unionize and the expansion of collective bargaining, in response to which the objections have come from employers.

Social Equity and Humanizing the Workplace

The next point I wanted to touch on is the subject of social equity. I will briefly mention aspects such as job maintenance, minimum wages, and training, although I have already referred to the latter. As you heard Minister Aninat and Minister Molina say yesterday, the subject of development and human capital in Chile is a crucial one. We are making a major effort in education, and we believe that a similar impetus should be given to training since it is clearly a factor that will contribute to fairer income distribution over the medium and long terms. What we at the Ministry of Labor see is that our national training system is largely filling in the gaps left by the educational system. Reforming secondary education should therefore have a significant indirect impact on the better and more appropriate use of our training resources. Our ongoing efforts to maintain high employment levels, a concern we share with the economic authorities, have been critical for social equity. This is because the impact of employment on individual or family poverty is extraordinarily great, which explains our perseverance in maintaining high employment rates, even in jobs that, in the vast domain of labor relations in Chile, are of low quality. Another challenge, of course, it to improve the quality of jobs, but at least we have jobs, and that is an important place to start. I should also mention that Chile has two minimum wages, which are required by law—one for workers in general and one for public employees. The latter is determined each year after negotiations with public sector employees' associations. For the government, the minimum wage is an instrument that, despite its difficulties and complexities, has an undeniably positive impact on social equity. The difficulties arise because some employers take the minimum wage set by law as *the* wage and tell their workers that this is what they are going to be paid. Of course, that was never the intention behind the minimum wage.

Finally, I would like to mention what have come to be known as policies to humanize the workplace. Fortunately, this subject is stimulating much discussion in Chile, although some people still see it as *poetry* or *fiction,* using those words with a negative connotation that I do not share. I think they are much more than that, and while some aspects are controversial, these are very specific policies that this ministry is promoting as another avenue of action. They include eradicating pockets of child labor in Chile, which, according to the United Nations, are very few in comparison with other countries. Nevertheless, we have signed an agreement with the ILO, joining the program to stamp out child labor, and will shortly establish a national committee to tackle this problem. We are going to work very hard in this area, in conjunction with the Ministry of Education, since we believe that our best weapon in preventing the exploitation of child labor is a solid, appealing, functional educational system.

We have also designed a series of policies regarding nondiscrimination in the workplace, particularly draft legislation and lines of action to prevent gender discrimination. In addition, we are developing a very active policy to reduce job-related accidents and improve safety in the workplace. Chile has had much success in this field in the last 25 to 30 years, with a significant reduction in accident rates. But, just as we have set a goal of single-digit inflation for the year 2000, we are determined to reduce the rate of accidents in the workplace to single-digits as well. This is a very desirable goal, especially for economic sectors that continue to experience high accident rates such as the construction, forestry, and fishing industries.

CHAPTER 12

Social Policy under the Frei Administration

Genaro Arriagada

In the past 18 years, Chile has undergone radical changes. Per capita GDP increased threefold between 1978 and 1995, meaning that in 1995 the average Chilean had access to three times more goods and services — or, to put it another way, was three times wealthier — than in 1978. The year 1996 marks 12 years of stable and steady economic growth averaging over 6 percent per annum. According to projections for growth over the 1996–2000 period, Chile will double its per capita GDP between 1990 and 2000 to about U.S.$6,050.

The Changing Face of Poverty

As a consequence of this burgeoning development, the visible face of poverty has changed: poverty is not an absolute. It is not the same to be poor in a country with per capita GDP of U.S.$1,420 (Chile in 1978) as in a country with per capita GDP of U.S.$6,050 (Chile in 2000). It is quite a different thing to be poor in a country with 60 percent illiteracy (Honduras in 1990) than in one with 5 percent illiteracy (Chile in 1990). Being poor in a country with 30 percent open unemployment (Chile in 1982) is a far cry from being poor in a country with 5.5 percent unemployment (Chile in 1995). Living in poverty under a dictatorship, without civil liberties or political freedom (Chile in 1973–89), is not like living in poverty in a democracy (Chile since 1990).

Given the circumstances prevailing in Chile, particularly since 1990, the phenomenon of poverty is markedly different today than it was 20, or even six, years ago. According to the CASEN survey, 28 percent of all Chileans were living in poverty in 1994. Today that percentage has dropped to an estimated 25 percent, but unemployment is only 5.5 percent. This means that the poor are working; the problem is not that there are no jobs but rather that the jobs available are not good ones. They lack job security and are low in productivity, which translates into low wages.

Chile today boasts virtually universal primary school enrollment, and high school enrollment is rising exponentially. A well-off family with a child in private school spends (invests) at least seven times more every month than the state spends for a child in the public education system. The opportunities open to these children in the future will be determined to some extent by the investment made in their education. The problem, then, is not the coverage of education but the unequal quality of education accessible to different children in what is essentially a two-tier system.

On the health care front, the main problem today is not the coverage of primary — or even secondary — services available. The main problem is the quality of care, which is marked by long waits, tardy secondary intervention, and condescending or indifferent service — again, second-class care for second-class citizens owing to an unequal distribution of quality care.

Studies performed in recent years by the Corporación de Promoción Universitaria (CPU) show that most Chileans feel defenseless when they receive ill treatment or their rights are violated. Access to justice is extremely limited, and the system is slow and cumbersome, all the more so for those with no money to pay lawyers' bills.

Collective bargaining is available to a very small percentage of workers in Chile today, and where it does exist the playing field is not level for workers and employers. Unemployment insurance is nonexistent, unionization is very difficult, and the labor movement is at its lowest ebb in the past 50 years. Meanwhile, business enjoys star status in terms of its bargaining power and its dialogue with the state and society.

What did poverty look like in 1975–76 or 1983–84? Poverty at that time meant squatter settlements, widespread hunger and communal soup kitchens, sky-high unemployment and government make-work programs, and too many children with no access to schools or health care. Fortunately, the country has changed, and, as the president said in his most recent address, poverty is no longer characterized by "widespread privation." But what is it like to be poor today?

We can talk about poverty on two levels. First we have the poorest of the poor, the indigent, who accounted for 8 percent of the population in 1994 according to the CASEN study and an estimated 6 percent in 1996. Then there are several million Chileans — perhaps as many as 40 to 50 percent of the population — who are poor in a different way. They consider themselves not as poor but as working class, impoverished middle class, or simply as families in need. How can we define the situation of these families?

The typical Chilean family in these circumstances can be described as follows:

First, the children go to elementary and secondary school but receive a mediocre education that does not equip them to take
advantage of opportunities on the horizon.

Second, the family has access to primary health care but must arrive
at the clinic at dawn and wait for hours to obtain service. They
will be allotted just 15 minutes, will frequently not be given adequate medical explanations, and will be subjected to harsh, over-
bearing treatment.

Third, any family member who needs surgery will have to wait for
months.

Fourth, if family members feel that their rights have been violated,
legal protection will not be forthcoming.

Last, but not least, the head of the household — and the spouse, if
working — have poor quality jobs with low productivity and low
pay.

The Social Policies of the Past

This new face of poverty calls for a revised social policy different from
those applied by the state in the past to build a more just society or at
least alleviate the rigors of poverty. During the first half of this century
and up to the early 1970s, Chile tried what we might call a Latin American version of the welfare state, a social policy that went hand in hand
with the import substitution model of development. The aim, and result,
of that policy was to shape Chilean society. This was done, inter alia, by
putting in place universal primary education and primary health care,
passing laws to protect workers and job security, bringing farmers and
their families into the mainstream through unionization and agrarian
reform, promoting civic participation by the urban poor, using tariffs to
protect national products and jobs, and helping the poor by placing price
controls on consumer staples.

In retrospect, this was a successful policy. Chile became one of the
most socially advanced countries of Latin America, with one of the
highest school enrollment rates on the continent and one of the best
health indicators in the region. Ours was an integrated and deeply democratic nation.

The institutional crisis of 1973 radically altered the model of economic growth and the political system, as well as putting an end to the
social policy model in place. Beginning in 1975, our country, almost as a
harbinger of what was to come elsewhere in the world, adopted a strin-
gent structural adjustment policy on the grounds that the import substitution model had outlived its usefulness. Among the measures adopted,

the economy was opened up to international trade, fiscal spending was cut back severely, and labor relations were made more flexible. The outcome of these drastic measures was social catastrophe. Real wages plummeted by 50 percent and unemployment skyrocketed to 30 percent (17 percent steady state). It became a real problem simply to obtain food and manage day to day life. Investments in health care, education, and housing were slashed, and both the numbers of the poor and the depth of poverty increased.

Against this backdrop emerged a second social policy, one that was intended to mitigate the high social cost of structural adjustment and drew its inspiration mainly from the neoliberalism of the 1980s. This was a social policy applied in tandem with structural adjustment and the new development model.

The new policy was predicated on targeting direct subsidies to those most in need in several identified areas. Implementing it meant gathering information on individual socioeconomic status — "CAS" (socioeconomic assessment certificate) files that distinguished five levels of poverty (extreme poverty was level 1). Subsidies could then be dispensed to specific individuals. This gave rise to aid programs such as family allowances (SUF), income supplements for pensioners (PASIS), and emergency employment programs such as Programa de Empleo Mínimo (PEM) and Programa de Empleo para Jefes de Hogar (POJH). Other subsidies — for health care (e.g., Programa Nacional de Alimentación Complementaria [PNAC] nutritional supplements), housing, child care, and school lunches — began to be paid on the basis of personal needs, as recorded in CAS files, or as refinements of the system in different agencies.

The main difference between the two policies was that the first established universal subsidies considered necessary to the nation as a whole, while the second provided direct, targeted subsidies to address the serious needs of individuals. Under the latter approach, scarce public funds dictated assisting only those most in need, the poorest of the poor, rather than middle-income groups. This approach ensured that those suffering most from the rigors of structural adjustment could find a way out of their straits with the help of effective and rational assistance provided through social spending by the state.

This social adjustment policy is well documented by Andrés Solimano in chapter 2 of this book. The policy he described is based on the following principles:

> Economic growth is the driving force behind reducing poverty and
>   improving living standards. Taken to its extreme, it is seen not
>   only as the driving force but as the only force. This is the neo-
>   liberal "trickle-down" theory.

Relative prices and market forces should determine the allocation of resources and provide incentives for saving and investment. Accordingly, social policies should be prevented from altering the economy's relative price structure with supply subsidies, which should be replaced with demand subsidies.

Social policies should be explicitly targeted to the more vulnerable population groups.

The private sector should be encouraged to take part in delivering and administering social services such as education and health care, and privatization and concession arrangements should be developed to this end.

The explicit and exclusive aim of this social policy is poverty reduction. Problems of economic and social disparity should not be the focus of public policy, the assumption being that such problems will be solved automatically through economic growth and the forces of the market.

A New Social Policy

The past is now behind us. The policies of the welfare state upon which some look back so fondly are no longer an appropriate response, nor are those promoted by the neoliberalism of the 1980s. The Chile of today, with 12 years of over 6 percent yearly growth to report and posting 6 percent unemployment with savings and investment on the order of 27 percent of GDP, is no longer a country in the throes of structural adjustment. Rather, we find ourselves on the verge of a new society: a post-adjustment society.

This begs the question of what is the appropriate policy for a country that paid the social toll of structural adjustment long ago and has per capita GDP of close to U.S.$5,000, a country in which the indigent account for a mere 6 percent of the population, unemployment stands at 6 percent, and coverage is virtually universal for education and health care services, even though quality may be second rate for two-thirds of the population.

The government's policy is apparent in two avenues of action. The first calls for upholding its unwavering commitment to indigent Chileans that extreme poverty will be eradicated. The second is to act on the basis that the key to the country's social development lies not there but in creating opportunities and building equity. The first avenue of action represents a fundamental moral commitment by the government, but it addresses only 6 percent of the population. The second is the cornerstone of the new social policy, since the challenge is no longer how to protect the victims of structural adjustment but how to extend to the entire population — particularly to the vast number of Chileans sandwiched between the indigent and the upper middle class — the opportunities available in Chile today. In other words, the great challenge is how to square sustained high growth with social equity, how to translate economic growth into building an ever more just, ever more integrated nation.

The great historic opportunity that lies before Chile today can be addressed in two different ways: either by offering the benefits of economic development to a privileged elite (20 to 25 percent of the population) or by extending it to all citizens. The essential belief of the coalition government (Concertación) is that this historic opportunity should be extended to all Chileans; this lies at the heart of its vision for the country. If the benefits associated with that opportunity are concentrated in a privileged elite, the Frei government and Concertación will have failed.

The major challenge now facing Chile has to do with the sharing of opportunity within society. That is the problem as stated by the government and forms the backbone of its social policy. Today's society, and tomorrow's even more so, is a society of opportunity, and it is widely acknowledged that the distribution of that opportunity within Chilean society is inequitable and highly concentrated. There are serious problems with making available opportunities for education, quality and equity in health care services, access to justice, employment and job training, and equity in labor relations.

The Concertación government has been working on this paradigm of opportunity and equity building since 1990. To some extent, social policy over the 1990–95 period has been a reflection, in the social sphere, of the Chilean transition, as new programs designed to create opportunities and improve equity have been superimposed on the traditional model of direct, individualized subsidies. These new social programs were initially incremental to those already in place and were quite modest, even marginal, in terms of budget commitments.

Today, however, marginal is no longer good enough. Intervention must go to the very heart of social policy. The time has come for a decisive change of direction away from concentrating opportunity in the hands of a few. Economic growth is the pillar upon which opportunities can be built. Strategies for economic growth driven by the market and international competitiveness have proved effective. Such a strategy has brought Chile 12 years of sustained expansion, and no other approach can hope to offer the country equivalent opportunities for economic advancement. A social policy model that creates opportunity and builds equity can be understood to operate in the framework of such a growth strategy.

President Frei has said that without economic growth it will be impossible to stamp out extreme forms of poverty and that stable and sustained growth, high investment and savings rates, low inflation, and low unemployment lay the best foundations and provide the best assurances for successfully combating poverty. The old populist policies of redistribution that thwart growth and investment, push up inflation, and bloat the fiscal deficit have been ruled out by the government as policies for social development.

Without economic growth there can be no new opportunities. But economic growth alone is no guarantee that opportunities will be available to all members of society equally. The government rejects the trickle-down theory as a basic tenet of social policy since it does not alter the distribution of opportunity. What is needed is a social policy that will be proactive, forceful, clear, and precise.

Here we must distinguish between two different phenomena. Unequal opportunity is one thing; the extreme forms of poverty — indigence or intractable poverty — are quite another. Inequality is a problem for between 60 and 85 percent of the population, depending on the variable in question. The aim is to build equity, a fairer sharing of opportunity, and to ensure that the great historic opportunity before us can be translated into real opportunities for all our citizens. Presently, 6 percent of Chile's people live in extreme poverty or indigence. Projections call for this figure to drop to 3 percent by the year 2000, assuming that current social policies are maintained. The government's goal is to eradicate extreme poverty by the year 2000.

Members of the business-oriented Right hold that public policy should be concerned solely with alleviating extreme poverty, addressing it through welfare-type subsidies, and that the concept of equity, as an ideological holdover from a statist past, has no place in public policy. Moreover, they claim that the state is particularly inefficient at solving the problems of extreme poverty and declare that if the government were prepared to privatize management of the problem (using tax incentives, for instance) the private sector could wipe out such poverty within a reasonably short time. On this point, the president has stated very clearly that the purpose of the government's public policy is as much to build equity as to overcome extreme poverty. And the government has no intention of privatizing poverty alleviation.

What is needed, then, are unequivocal policies and programs to address the problems of equity as well as extreme poverty and to rank them by priority.

The policy on equity building has three aspects:

Passing on available opportunities to all the country's citizens and ensuring that the benefits of growth and modernization reach all citizens as well. This means not allowing opportunities and benefits to accrue exclusively to a privileged elite.

Equipping the majority of Chileans with the tools to take advantage of opportunities as they arise. It is not enough merely to know that the opportunities are there; having access to them is essential. In a society of opportunity, the basic tool is the entrepreneurial spirit, which must inform educational reform, new forms of job training, policies to promote small business and microenterprise, and so on.

Rewriting the relationship between public services and their users, putting an end to the sociocultural phenomenon of discrimination against the poor. Modernizing the public administration quickly and urgently will be a key policy element in ending differential treatment of people as first- or second-class citizens.

The equity-building policy focuses on the family. It is no longer needy individuals but Chilean families that will benefit from the flow of opportunities. The aim is to have an ordinary family of four in which the children receive an education just as good as that of a child in the wealthiest 20 percent of the population; the mother can take her children to a neighborhood clinic and be served with respect and dignity; a medical condition requiring secondary care will be treated quickly, efficiently, and with respect; job training is available to boost productivity and pay; living space includes green areas, better housing, and safety; and public services are provided rapidly and efficiently in a dignified and respectful manner. The list could go on. The point is not to find an individual with a specific need in order to dispense the appropriate subsidy but to provide a flow of diverse opportunities to all families so that they may advance as the country advances.

When it comes to equity-building policy, the idea of targeting individuals no longer applies. The idea is rather to target programs. The key to evaluation is not to ask whether the subsidy reached the poorest of the poor but whether a particular program is an efficient way of providing most of the country's population with opportunities for advancement. For instance, the nation requires a public education system that can offer quality education, and therefore opportunities for the future, to all children served by the public system. The same applies to health care, justice, housing, self-employment, and so on.

Policies to address extreme poverty (6 percent of the population) should continue to be welfare based in conception and targeted in operation. Very specific information is needed as to what kinds of programs are efficient and effective in both rural and urban areas. The revolution implied by the mass implementation of opportunity programs will necessarily have a positive effect on the extremely poor (e.g., by extending classroom hours). The point is that it is also necessary to apply direct subsidies to help these people deal with the conditions of extreme poverty in which they live.

Strategic Areas of Intervention under the New Model

Education

It is universally accepted today that education is the key to opening up horizons in areas as diverse as personal development, productivity, access to better jobs, social and labor mobility, and equal opportunity. Education is the master key to gaining access to opportunities arising in the future. Intervention is needed throughout the public school system to extend classroom hours and introduce mass programs to improve quality.

Improving the Quality of Jobs and Productivity

The way to improve living conditions is by providing access to better quality jobs that call for higher productivity. Most of the Chilean labor force is employed, but many jobs are poorly paid and not unionized, with no security or collective bargaining. Policies to raise productivity, provide job training, and promote labor advancement, balance, and equity in labor relations are thus a particularly important focus. People will gradually overcome poverty and join the mainstream as they become able to live a decent life with opportunities for advancement and reasonable pay.

Placing Public Servants at the Service of the People

Many Chilean families are obliged to call upon public services repeatedly to solve problems in their daily lives. In these contacts, they often encounter excessive red tape and are treated rudely. This is apparent on a daily basis in the area of health care, but the same problem arises in connection with any number of day to day dealings. In practice, this means that people are treated like second-class citizens. Programs to modernize the state and public services are therefore crucial to serving people with dignity and respect, quickly and efficiently, with just as much entitlement as citizens belonging to the wealthiest 20 percent of society.

Equal Access to Justice

A high proportion of Chileans today lack access to legal protection when their rights are trampled. When they do gain access to the justice system, the proceedings are cumbersome and lengthy and ultimately fail to solve the problem. Bringing the legal system within the reach of the people and updating judicial processes are also essential to instilling more equity in society.

Fostering Business Skills among Microentrepreneurs

What microentrepreneurs need, more than subsidies to provide them with a protected existence, are productive development tools that will make them economically viable and able to produce more and better goods and services, obtain better pay for their work, contribute more to the national economy, and thus invest self-employment with dignity.

A Decent Habitat: Promoting Social Mobility through Access to Housing

Low-income families are currently "assigned" to a particular type of housing in substandard living environments with no possibility of moving up the housing ladder. They therefore lack the freedom to choose their own surroundings.

Let me finish with a brief digression. The social situation in Chile is quite satisfactory compared to most of the rest of the world. The numbers of the poor and indigent have plunged since 1990. A recent ECLAC study (*Fifteen Years of Economic Performance*) indicates that, among all the countries in the region, only Chile and Uruguay have managed to reduce poverty to precrisis levels, and only Chile and Colombia have improved on the situation prevailing in the 1980s in terms of both urban employment and real wages (until 1997).

Chile has seen 12 years of uninterrupted economic growth topping 6 percent per annum, declining unemployment, rising real wages, and a remarkable drop in the number of those living in poverty, from 44.6 percent in 1987 to 26 percent in 1995. Still, there is no denying the frail social underpinnings of this model of economic growth. You have just published a survey showing that 55 percent of the population views the economic model as unfair.

It is urgent, therefore, that we — and you as a government — apply our best efforts to pursuing our aims: economic globalization, technological progress, capital market development, and further strides in productivity. But we need to make as much or more of an effort to come up with a social policy that will give the state and public policy an active role in overcoming poverty, narrowing the appalling gap between rich and poor, creating jobs, relieving the insecurity experienced by too many workers, and, above all, genuinely and effectively creating equal opportunity.

Contributors

Eduardo Aninat	Minister of Finance, Santiago, Chile
José Pablo Arellano	Minister of Education, former Budget Director, Santiago, Chile
Jorge Arrate	Minister, Secretary General of Government, Santiago, Chile
Genaro Arriagada	Chilean Ambassador to the United States, former Minister Secretary of the Presidency, Chile
Nancy Birdsall	Former Executive Vice President, Inter-American Development Bank, Carnegie Endowment for International Peace, Washington, DC, USA
Michael Bruno†	Chief Economist and Senior Vice President, Development Economics, World Bank, Washington, DC, USA
Julie Clugage	World Bank, Washington, DC, USA
Kevin Cowan	Massachusetts Institute of Technology, Cambridge, MA
José De Gregorio	Universidad de Chile, Santiago, Chile
Sergio Molina	Former Minister of Education, Chile, Banco del Desarrollo, Santiago, Chile
Martin Ravallion	World Bank, Washington, DC, USA
Andrés Solimano	World Bank, Washington, DC, USA
Lyn Squire	World Bank, Washington, DC, USA
Barbara Stallings	Economic Commission for Latin America and the Caribbean, United Nations, Santiago, Chile
Vito Tanzi	International Monetary Fund, Washington, DC, USA
Lance Taylor	New School for Social Research, New York, NY, USA

Index